That's That

That's That

My Life Story

Howard Hershberger

iUniverse, Inc.
Bloomington

That's That
My Life Story

iUniverse books may be ordered through booksellers or by contacting:

iUniverse
1663 Liberty Drive
Bloomington, IN 47403
www.iuniverse.com
1-800-Authors (1-800-288-4677)

ISBN: 978-1-4620-2131-4 (sc)
ISBN: 978-1-4620-2132-1 (ebk)

Printed in the United States of America

iUniverse rev. date: 05/25/2011

To
My loving wife Martha and our dearly loved children,
grandchildren and great grandchildren:

John, Chris, Daniel, Marla, Philip, Diana, Faith, Tim,
Beth, Mark, Jana, Julie, Joe, Laura, Brent, Micah, Sarah,
Saundra, Ben, Jessica H, Jessica P, Sam, Daniel, Annalie,
Olivia, Felicity, Christian, Thomas and all those who follow
after.

CONTENTS

Preface

In writing this document my wife Martha observed I put a plethora of "that's" in the text which she largely edited out. When explaining this to pastor Kurt Horst he jokingly suggested calling the manuscript That's That. The title resonated with me so it became the title for the story, thanks to Kurt. Many years ago I facetiously told Heber Ramer I was going to name the manuscript (if I ever wrote it) "Beyond Maturity" but it has now taken second billing and become the title for my last chapter. During the past year we have met with Walt and Carol Friesen for breakfast each week and Walt has shared some of his writings about growing up in western Kansas. During the summer of 2010 Martha and I visited my homes in Alberta, where I grew up. There just seemed to be some stories needing to be told from the time which seems light years away from the current scene. In the fall of 2010 we visited the birthplace and growing up communities of Walt Friesen in western Kansas which so closely paralleled my own. It was the final spark to light the fire of putting down my own pilgrimage.

My story is in no way spectacular but it is peculiarly my own. I am the only one who walked this specific journey. Particular thanks go to Martha who read and reread the manuscript and cheered me on when I was unsure the story was worthwhile and contemplated quitting. She has been the person who has always stood by me through good times and bad, when I needed encouragement and when I needed reining in. Very singular thanks goes to Bill Zuercher who knows the English language in a way I only dream of and went through the manuscript with a fine tooth comb for spelling, punctuation and grammar without disturbing the way I like to express myself. I also need to thank Walt Friesen and daughter Faith Penner who contributed to content ideas and items which should be included and some which shouldn't.

I wish I could name all of the wonderful friends who have faithfully stood by us during these many years. There are too many to enumerate and if I tried there would still be important ones who would have been left out.

That's That

I enjoyed asking questions so I asked, "If everyone is so sad, why are we moving to Mazeppa?" A quiet sadness hung over everyone in the car and my mother was softly crying. No one gave me a satisfactory answer so we continued on our journey in cheerless silence while I read my book. It was November 27, 1935, my ninth birthday, and Grandpa and Grandma Brenneman had gone to Edmonton with my parents and all of my siblings. We had lunch together and Grandpa gave me a book, *The Great Healer,* as a birthday present and had inscribed it. Grandpa and Grandma treated us to an early lunch in a café. We said our goodbyes and headed south to Mazeppa in our 1928 Chevrolet. There were seven of us in the car: my parents, Glenn who was fourteen, Pearl eleven, myself newly nine, James six, and John four.

(Mom and Dad – 1920)

My father had accepted a call as a self-supporting pastor to the Mt. View congregation in rural High River, Alberta. This was a monumental move for us. My parents lived on a very nice farmstead, owned by my grandfather, and farmed 640 acres of land. We were surrounded by a host of uncles, aunts and cousins as well as more distant relatives on my mother's side of the family.

The congregation we were a part of was Salem Mennonite Church, at Tofield, Alberta. It was a thriving congregation comprised almost entirely of United States transplants, primarily from the Milford, Nebraska area. The John Stauffer family, my Grandma Barbara's family, had all moved

to Alberta during a short period of time between 1912 and 1915, two brothers and six sisters with their families. They moved with money and had immediately built nice farmsteads in the rural Tofield area. Grandpa Brenneman had moved to Nebraska from Ontario in

(Grandpa Brenneman family – 1921)

1897 when he was twenty-one years old. He soon found Barbara Stauffer and they set out to raise a family.

My father had come to Alberta from Missouri in 1918 to avoid the draft in the United States and had gone to work as a farmhand for Milo Stutzman, one of the pastors of the Salem church. It was there he met my mother and they were married on March 4, 1920 at her parents' home. Because my mother was needed in the home to care for her six brothers and one sister, they lived with my grandparents for the first year. During that time my grandmother and mother were both expecting; Grandma gave birth to Uncle Paul in December and my brother Glenn was born in February. I believe my parents moved to their new home two miles north of my grandparents' home in 1921 or 1922. They had an excellent set of buildings, all painted white. This included a full two-story house, a large hip-roof barn, a chicken house, hog house, granary, garage and machine shed. This 640 acre farm was owned by my grandpa and I never heard of any plans for my parents to take ownership. I believe Grandpa wanted to control it as he did all of his other farms.

The Tofield years (1926-35)

It was on this farm I came into the world on November 27, 1926. The local doctor came out from Riley for the delivery. I'm not sure how he would have been notified since we did not have a phone except for a private line to my grandparents' house two miles down the road. It could be my grandparents were called and in turn they, who had a phone to the outside world, contacted the doctor. I'm sure my grandmother was also present at the delivery. I weighed in at ten pounds at birth and have been

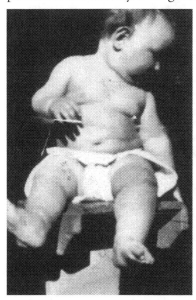

(Baby Howard – 1927)

slightly overweight ever since. I was the fourth child born but my brother Kenneth, the second child, died from scarlet fever at six months. I turned out to be the middle child, being followed by James in 1929 and John in 1931.

I believe I was a bit of a pet of my grandfather's because whenever I had a new pair of overalls he would need to take the *"schneider"* (German for tailor) out of them. This consisted of putting me over his knee and giving me a series of swats on the behind. I never heard my grandfather laugh out loud but he would silently shake while the tears rolled down his cheeks when he was highly amused. Before I went to grade school I would regularly ride with him in his truck during harvesting and grain hauling. He would buy me ten cents worth of licorice or Scottish mints for my refreshment and enjoyment. Although he was a very successful farmer, builder and manager he was not a great mechanic. The radiator on his truck was leaking so to keep from adding water he put in some *Sunny Boy,* a common cooked cereal of the area. This temporarily plugged the leak but apparently he put a little too much in and it blew up over everything including some on him. He laughed, "I guess I fed it too much Sunny Boy."

We always went to church twice on Sunday no matter what the weather was like. In the wintertime it was by sleigh. My father, along with

a number of our other neighbors, had taken a junk car body and mounted it on sleigh runners. The reins were extended through the windshield which could be cranked outward to provide some windbreak but allowed the horses to be controlled, most of the time. We would pile on

(Dad, Mom & children with Model T)

the blankets and quite often heat large rocks in the oven to place on the floor of the car body. Thus equipped we would head off for church, seven

miles away. On the way home the rocks were only cold rocks so we mostly shivered until we reached home.

Singing in church, while sitting beside my father, is still a special memory. He had a good tenor voice and I would very proudly sit beside him and try to emulate his sound. He quite often led the

(Car body on runners with Glenn at the controls with siblings and Bimbo the sheep)

congregational singing and used a tuning fork to get the pitch. I believe the fork was tuned to middle C and using that as the basis for the pitch

4

would then modulate to the pitch the song was written in. He also helped in singing school which was designed to help persons learn the scales and note values. The song books were all in shaped notes so we learned the do, re, mi's from the shapes of the notes. Even though I learned the notes by position later in life I still enjoy seeing shaped notes. He would also participate in special music on occasion but it was not a normal occurrence to have special music on any given Sunday.

I do not have many memories of Sunday school but I have many memories of the congregation meeting in corporate worship. The men always sat separate from the women—the men on the north or the right side of the church and the women on the south or the left side. Years later when we moved to Hesston and attended the Pennsylvania Mennonite Church the men still sat on the north side of the church but since it had a different orientation the men were now on the left side and the women on the right. How did they decide which side to sit on when they built a new church? I have not seen anything about this issue in any church doctrine book I have read!

I remember a Sunday morning when a young unmarried couple got up in church to confess she was pregnant and they were asking for the forgiveness of the church. I never forgot the event and every time I saw that couple I remembered them standing in front of the church. Since my memory bank never got cleared of the event I have often wondered if there wasn't a better way to deal with the issue than making such a public airing of the transgression. I was probably seven years old at the time. It has reminded me of the impressions left very early in life, when we probably don't realize little eyes are watching and observing.

(Howard, Glenn and Pearl)

One Sunday the Sunday school superintendent, Harold Lauber, confessed to the sin of pride in front of the whole congregation. It was in connection with the Sunday school lesson but was a legitimate confession on his part. Later on that day, when we were visiting at one of the congregational homes, I overheard some adults talking about this event and wondering aloud what he had to be proud about. I realized again, at an age of not more than seven, some things are just not safe to share in front of the whole congregation. It should be said in the defense of my parents that they were not party to that conversation and would not have been.

James J. Bucher, was a visiting evangelist from Oregon. I was not quite eight years old at the time and James J. was preaching as only he could. He was a prophecy student and had large charts and maps on the front of the church. I remember one of his stories about an individual who had asked them for a ride someplace and he informed the questioner, "You're welcome to come along but if we're going down the road and the Lord returns this old car is going to leave the road and crash and I'm going home to glory." I don't know if the person inquiring went with him or not but I remember the word picture of his car leaving the road. He had many other stories like this that made me *very* uneasy so I decided that I was sick. My parents seemed to understand and let me sit in the car for a couple evenings. It was a little stronger meat than I was prepared for. I'm not sure if it left any irreparable psychological damage or not. Others can make that call. Many years later when I was visiting in Oregon, the above-mentioned Brother Bucher was in a retirement home and was causing a problem because he couldn't keep his hands off one of the female residents.

I also have a memory of my great uncle, by marriage, Milton Martin, singing at the Salem church. He lived in Oregon and on the way to Alberta had a wreck. He stood in front of the church with his head swathed in bandages and sang "I dreamed that the great judgment morning had dawned." I thought he had a good voice. It definitely was a dramatic presentation. Years later when our quartet was in Oregon I realized my boyhood impression was not wrong. He led the congregational singing and indeed had an excellent voice.

One Sunday evening in late spring we were going to church and noticed the weather was very threatening. We had started to church early and stopped at grandpa's on the way. We were all standing in the kitchen looking out the north window where we thought the primary storm clouds were gathering. Suddenly Pearl, who was standing in the kitchen looking south, shouted, "Oh, look at Grandpa's barn!" The top of the barn had been completely blown away as well as the forty-foot windmill that stood beside it. The tornado that struck strewed the debris completely across

(At grandpa's place with uncles, aunts and cousins – 1935)

the section of land to the east. Even though he didn't have insurance, the following summer the barn was rebuilt and a new windmill erected. It was a fun time to observe the rebuilding. Clarence "Speed" Brenneman from Oregon, who had been a student at Hesston, helped in the rebuilding and during the shingling process got a hatchet in his forehead. He survived but had a nasty scar that lasted his lifetime.

Uncle Joe was my favorite uncle and from very early I was following him around like a little puppy. He had a great sense of humor and enjoyed teasing me and everyone else that came into his path. He named me Izador Rosenbloom, a moniker that I still use in various forms for a computer password. I have no idea where he came up with the name but it seemed to fit. He was a very diligent worker—no one could sow straighter rows of wheat or haul bigger or better formed loads of bundles at harvest time. Harvest was a special time for me and before I started first grade I would follow him at harvest time hauling bundles. One time I was observing that one of the hired men was not hauling nearly as big or well-formed loads as Uncle Joe so I asked him "Why doesn't he haul big loads like you do?" He replied "Why don't you ask him?" So I did. Not necessarily the best advice I ever received!! The poor hired hand went into a funk. I believe it eventually led to his termination. I was always a little diffident about joining the harvest hands at my aunt's bountiful harvest table because the men used to tease me about whether I had earned my keep or not. I knew

I hadn't but couldn't resist the food. None of my other cousins ever joined in my preoccupation with the harvesting process. I would sometimes take a three-tined pitch fork and pretend I was pitching bundles for play time. We had a team of Percheron horses called Prince and Beulah. I would ask Uncle Joe, "Is Prince older than Beulah, or is Beulah older than Prince?" I don't remember the answer!

I would follow Uncle Joe wherever he went. In October of 1933 he married Grace Plank and they built a small house right in Grandpa's front yard. Suddenly I realized I could no longer follow Uncle Joe everywhere. He had another first priority. I knew, without being told, that I no longer could walk with him into his home without being invited in like I did when he lived at Grandma's house. He still remained my hero but not long after he was married we moved out of the community so those special times were gone. He would affectionately call Aunt Grace, Mrs. Gallagher. She didn't seem to like it overly well but that didn't keep him from calling her that anyway. I later adopted Mrs. Gallagher as my pet name for Martha.

(Dad with McCormick-Deering 15-30)

Another significant uncle was Paul. In many ways he was more like an older brother since he provided primary entertainment for his nephews and nieces. Although Glenn and Paul were the same age they had entirely different interests. Paul was the youngest child in his family and Glenn was the oldest in his. Glenn usually was engaged with the older folks and Paul, with an entourage of nephews and nieces, played all kinds of games. He also built a scale model of an entire farmstead in the back of their garden. The house and barn were about four feet tall. It was also from Uncle Paul I developed an interest in sports and cars. Grandpa always had a good car. Later, when we lived at Mazeppa, Grandpa and Grandma Brenneman with Uncle Paul and Aunt Norma stopped at our place on their way back to Tofield from Detroit with a new 1937 Buick. It was a classy rig. Perhaps that is why I have enjoyed Buicks for most of my adult life and have owned a number of them. Uncle Paul, many years later, with Aunt Grace, provided a home away from home for our children when they were at school in the east. It was a particular blessing to our family.

We regularly had hired men during the harvesting season and quite often during other times as well. The long-term hired men were young men from our church who needed employment and their parents either didn't have extra farm land or already had other children who could do the work. I always enjoyed the young men who lived and worked at our place. They were usually very good workers and I learned responsible work habits from them as well as from my uncles. The hired men that we brought in for harvest were not quite as good role models. One time my mother had gone to Tofield to pick up several men at the local hotel. The hotel was the place in town where they served liquor but was where the men congregated for work assignments. Mother picked three men up but they were quite inebriated and were vomiting so they would ask my mother to stop so they could vomit but there was always one left in the car. Mother said that she would have driven off if all three of them had gotten out at once. The next day they were all returned to Tofield.

We always had a twenty-two caliber rifle that was hung on the wall in the hallway. This was used for shooting game or killing animals for butchering. My mother never touched the gun but she had been noticing that some of her little chicks were disappearing from the chicken coop. She suspected a predator was taking them. One day she noticed a hawk perched on the fence post just outside the chicken coop. She picked the gun off the rack, inserted a bullet into the chamber, and from a distance of at least 150 feet fired a shot the hawk never heard. He dropped like a hammer. When we went out to look we found that she had shot the hawk right through its head. Having a perfect record she retired from her hunting exploits and never picked the gun up again.

My parents did most of their serious shopping in Edmonton, a city about forty-five miles away. One time when I was about three or four they took us all over to Uncle Harvey's place for the day while they went to Edmonton. Their well for drinking water was out about a hundred feet from the house and Aunt Uarda took a pail to get water for kitchen use. The children all followed her out to the pump with little Howard bringing up the rear. Maurice Yoder from Hesston College was holding a series of meetings at the Salem church and Uncle Titus, with my grandpa's car, was driving him around to visit the congregants. They had been visiting Uncle Harvey and Aunt Uarda and were backing up to leave. He noticed Aunt Uarda with a group of children had passed behind the car but didn't notice me behind the rest of the group and he backed completely over me. I passed safely between the wheels and only suffered a gash on my head where the bumper had knocked me down. I don't remember exactly what happened right after the event but I remember my mother making a lot of fuss over me that evening after they had returned from their day trip. She told me I could have been killed to which I nonchalantly replied, "But I wasn't."

Since we did not have electricity we would store ice from the winter to last for the summer months. The men would harvest ice from Beaver Lake, now a dry lake, when the ice was about two or three feet thick and haul it by sleigh to our place. We had dug a hole just north of our house about ten feet deep and perhaps eight feet square. The hole was lined with lumber similar to a foundation form and a lid placed over it. The ice was cut into blocks about eighteen inches square and lowered into the hole with sawdust placed between the blocks to keep them from freezing together. This supplied us with ice for cooling foodstuff that needed refrigeration. It was also used for making ice cream during the summer months. I always enjoyed these special occasions.

A very extraordinary time was butchering. Pork was the red meat of preference on the farm. Butchering was a community event (meaning the Brenneman community.) They would set up a tripod about ten feet high and after killing the pig would lift it by block and tackle to the apex of the tripod for gutting and processing. The hog was always scalded so they could scrape all of the hair off before processing the meat. This was an important part of the process because if you "didn't get a good scald," getting the carcass clean was considerably more difficult. Getting something done correctly is still in my vocabulary as "a good scald." Uncle Harvey was the main man in charge of the butchering process. I remember distinctly how he would prepare himself and the utensils for cutting up the meat. Everything had to be sterilized. He would scrub like he was preparing for surgery and then had everyone put a bandanna on their heads to keep hair from falling into the meat. Cracklings, the residue left over from the processing of lard, were a special treat when they were still hot, although one didn't need too many of them before you knew you had enough.

Fresh liver was served at the noon meal for the crew. I still like liver and onions. Cleaning the casings for the sausage was also an interesting process and was usually handled by the women. The intestines were emptied and thoroughly rinsed out and then water was run through them. Then they were completely emptied by tying two steel knitting needles together at one end and by applying pressure at the other end the intestines were pulled between the needles to completely drain them. I hope they were clean—if they weren't at least the sausage was always cooked before eating! Butchering day always ended by feeling most everything was right in my little world.

I have no recollection of either of my two younger brothers being born or expecting them to be born. I have since commiserated about that gap in my memory. From older cousin Roderick and uncles I learned the essentials about the birds and the bees. I had no knowledge that my mother was even pregnant. I think we got shuttled off to one of the relatives the day of the event and when we got home there was another child in the family. Another reason I might have missed both of their births was because both of them were born during harvest season when I had more important agenda. James was almost three years younger than me and John five years younger.

My mother often helped with the milking when I was small. One evening when our parents, and probably Glenn, were out milking after supper, Pearl and I were doing the dishes. She was washing and I was drying. We had a hutch cabinet with dishes in the top and on the base of the unit our drinking water supply in a three gallon pail. The pail had a ladle that we collectively used to supply ourselves with water. On the top of this hutch was a kerosene lamp to give light to the kitchen. The evening of this particular event I was putting the dishes away as I finished drying. I was too short to reach the glass doors on the upper cabinet so I grabbed the handle to boost myself onto the cabinet base. I applied too much force and the whole upper part of the cabinet came crashing down on me; the kerosene lamp came down, the dishes lay broken all over the floor, and the contents from the bucket of water immersed it all. I escaped serious injury and Pearl ran out to the barn to inform my parents about what had happened. My parents didn't punish me. They recognized that I was trying to do the right thing and had only exercised poor judgment. Perhaps if it had happened again it would have been a different story but I was properly

11

penitent and they recognized it. Everyone felt relieved there was no fire since the lamp was burning when it made its descent.

Living in the cold climate of the north we experienced lots of cold and snow during the winter months. On a very cold morning when I was in the first grade during the Christmas season my father took us to school in the homemade bobsled. I could not find one of

(Children and homemade sled)

my mittens and everyone was getting on my case because they were ready to go and I wasn't. It was not an unusual occasion for me to misplace something and part of the pressure I was getting from my siblings was because of it. Finally in exasperation I said I would go with just one mitten and put the hand without the mitten in my pocket. We arrived at school and noticed the teacher was there so my father returned home and we went into the school. Hennie Aniboe, our teacher said, "Oh didn't you know we aren't having school today?" No, we didn't know we weren't having school so we headed home, a two mile walk. There is disagreement about the story between my sister Pearl and me because she said our teacher took us part way home in her sleigh and my recollection is we walked the whole way. The part there is no disagreement on is by the time we got home my hand was completely frozen. I remember trailing Glenn and Pearl with my bare hand sticking out because I said "It's no colder outside than in my pocket." When we got home my father took snow and rubbed my hand until it thawed out. It was the conventional wisdom of that time. It hurt like blazes when it was thawing out but the hand never got sore and appeared to have completely recovered. It was not until later it was discovered the three outside fingers on my left hand did not grow normally beyond the last two joints. It always remained functional but the ends were stubby and the finger nails were only half the length of my right hand nails.

The coldest I ever saw was fifty-eight degrees below zero. I remember walking outside very heavily bundled and the cold burning my nostrils. It was completely calm and the snow crunched loudly when I walked on it. It didn't take long for me to decide inside was the best place for me.

Our father did most of the reading to us. He enjoyed doing it and mama enjoyed having him do it. Because of the long winter evenings we needed entertainment and without the world only a knob away we had to make our own. Pearl's favorite time was having music

(Pearl, John, Glenn, James and Howard)

lessons while Glenn and I wanted Bible stories. Stories usually won out. My father was an excellent reader and he made the Bible stories come alive. The book of choice was *Hurlbut's Story of the Bible*. I knew the Bible stories in a way that was a source of frustration to some of my friends when later I took Bible History at Hesston Academy. Ivan Lind was the teacher and he graded on the curve and posted all of the grades. It was no contest. Thanks to Dad I aced the course. One of my special heroes was Jonathan, David's special friend. I'm not sure why I identified with him but I was struck with how he promoted David when *he* was the son of the king.

Another habit that my father had was memorizing scripture; he would pick a verse and repeat it many times during the week. We couldn't help but memorize them ourselves. The next week would be another verse or group of verses. He kept the verses in a little card file marked *Daily Bread*.

We had a dam behind the barn that collected water from a draw that went next to our farm. Water accumulated in this and served as a watering hole for the farm animals during the summer and a skating pond during the winter. It also was a bathing hole the few times it was warm enough to get in the water. One day, before I was of school age, I was down with my brother Glenn wading in the pond. The mosquitoes which are usually plentiful in an Alberta summer were particularly bad that day and took me on as their special project. I was completely covered with welts and I went crying up to the house naked and unashamed with my body on fire. My mother put lots of baking soda on my welts and I was soon back to normal. A lasting benefit that I received from the episode is although mosquitoes still bite me occasionally they have never become welts on my skin. I believe I got inoculated that day for mosquito bites.

Eating has always been an important part of my life and there are two particular events that stand out in my mind. One was good and one not so good. We had been invited by a church family for an evening meal. This family was one that was a bit marginalized by the larger community and their food offering was not quite up to the standards I was used to. There was a big pot of chicken pieces in a heavy stew being passed. I dug in, but since the stew was heavy, I was unable to see what I was getting. Much to my dismay I pulled out a chicken leg with claws attached. It did present a challenge to me but I think I kept my mother from being too embarrassed with me. I ate most of it. The other eating experience was when we were invited to our Lutheran neighbors, the Eriksons. This was a bit unusual because although we were friendly neighbors we did not break bread with them. The elder Erikson was a widower but his son Carl had married a nicely-turned-out lady and lived on the farm with his father. We were invited to a Thanksgiving dinner that was prepared by the young Mrs. Erikson. We had turkey, dressing and cranberry salad; the latter was a completely new dish to me. The cranberries were very coarsely ground and were deliciously tart. I was hooked on cranberries although seldom had them until I married and now Martha prepares them just as good as Mrs. Erikson did in 1933.

School at the old Amish Creek School was a bit mixed. The English system of education in Canada provided for nine grades of schooling in grade school. The older boys were sometimes a problem and there seemed to be very little supervision on the playground. Marvin Moen was a ninth grade bully who was a fight promoter and enjoyed pitting little kids against each other. We would fight regularly, usually without serious consequences but it sometimes got a little out of hand. Whereas I thought I might be Grandpa's pet, I soon found out I was Marvin Moen's favorite tormentee. I had rather large ears and he would grab me and chew my ears saying, "I'm going to chew your little ears off." They weren't little but they did survive the abuse. Our road home overlapped with his for about a mile and a half and one day during the spring thaw he decided it would be fun to torment me by hanging me by the heels over the bridge banister of a raging creek. He lowered me until my hands touched the water then he brought me back up. I have no knowledge of whether my parents found out about that or not. I was delighted when he left school for other pursuits. We moved away during my second year of school and I never saw him again.

The Bob Bergs were other Lutheran neighbors. They had a very nice farmstead just across the section and we could see his fine house and large red-roofed barn from our place. One day he hung himself in his barn. I had no idea why he did that since he seemed like a very good man to me. It was not talked about at our dinner table. For this eight-year-old boy it was a most traumatic event. Why did he do it and what would I do if my father did it? From that time on probably for almost a year I kept watch over my Dad like a hawk. I would sometimes go to my parents' room at night to see if they were still in bed. My parents asked me what was wrong but I was unable to frame a reply. From my perspective there was no reason why our friendly and happy neighbor would take his life so how could I be sure my father wouldn't do the same! Even though I outgrew the fear by the time we moved to Mazeppa it wasn't until I became an adult that I shared those early fears with my father.

We lived in a very social church community. It seemed like almost every Sunday we either were company or had company. This was usually outside of the immediate family and there always seemed to be a gang—usually three tables full. The men always ate first, the women second, and the children last. Now that I am an old man I observe that the children are first, the women second and the men last. We children always had a good time even though we were powerfully hungry by the time our turn came. I also got to observe which hostesses were the most efficient at getting the meal on the table. Because of this socialization when we went back to Alberta in 2010 I was able to locate most of the farmsteads of the congregation after being gone for seventy-five years with only a few visits between.

In 1935 the Salem congregation decided to call one of their own as an additional pastor. There was a congregational vote and my father received a majority of the votes but the custom was for the decision to be made by lot. In this case it consisted of the four highest vote recipients. The evening of the vote we were at Grandpa and Grandma's house for supper but Grandpa didn't come to the table because it was said that he was fasting and praying concerning the lot that evening. The evening meeting was a very solemn occasion with a full house. There were four song books on the communion table in the front. The candidates each came forward and picked a book and the bishop, Isaac Miller, opened each book being held by the candidate to a certain page where a slip of paper had been inserted with a scripture verse on it. The lot fell on J. B. Stauffer, one of the more unlikely candidates. It should be noted that some years later he was chosen as a bishop by the same process. Although not a very dynamic speaker he seemed to have served well.

Shortly after this event, Isaac Miller asked my father if he would consider coming to the Mt. View congregation near High River to serve as pastor and assist him in the church leadership. It remains a mystery to this day why he did not have to go through the lot process and was not even chosen by a congregational vote of the Mt. View congregation, to my knowledge. This also was a mystery to my mother who was a bit cynical of the whole process. My father, who felt called to the ministry, after some deliberation and after a visit to the area agreed to accept the call to High River. We then prepared to make the move.

I left the Tofield years with some questions. Why are we moving to Mazeppa when no one seems to want to go? Why did a seemingly happy man take his own life? Is Prince older than Beulah?

Musings on the Tofield years

Now, seventy-five years after the events, and having attended many family reunions of the Jacob Brenneman family, I have some thoughts about those years. In many ways I had an idyllic childhood. I grew up surrounded by loving parents, grandparents, uncles and aunts and a strong church community. I have been blest.

My father came up to Alberta to avoid the draft during the First World War. He married into probably the most powerful family in the area. Because my Uncle Harvey had been a problem son, joining the military and then being redeemed by Grandpa and then marrying an English girl, Uarda Hill, he lost some of the rights of the firstborn. The prime farm of the number owned by my grandfather was given to the second child, my mother, to live on and farm. My father seemed to be completely accepted into the larger family but I do know the Brenneman sons were very competitive. After we moved to High River, Uncle Harvey and Aunt Uarda moved into the home we vacated since by that time he was completely back in the fold of the family and the church. My father and Uncle Harvey jointly owned some equipment. It seemed like a very amicable arrangement and I never heard any words about either the finances or the usage of the equipment.

Father was very well respected in the church and community and was a capable farmer who had a strong work ethic. It is possible that he was getting a little weary of being under the control of Grandpa Brenneman. It is also possible that his willingness to leave and move to an economically depressed area with only half the amount of farm land and eke out a living in a new community was mostly altruistic (he was a good man.) Our relationship had always been cordial with the larger family and that never changed. Mother seemed to be the biggest loser in the move. She was surrounded by a lot of women her age who were good friends in addition to her immediate family.

It seemed also, in retrospect, that our move started a process of thinking by mother's siblings that maybe it was okay to leave the enclave and move out on their own. As mentioned earlier, there did not seem to be an interest on the part of my grandparents to relinquish control and ownership of the farms to their children. It was not until Grandfather died in 1946 that the children received the farm land. The family started exiting in the early 40s and by the mid 1940s Norma was the only child of the original family that still resided in Alberta.

My Hershberger Family

Because we lived 2000 miles from Father's family we did not get to see them very often. Father was the oldest son and fourth child of a family of four boys and four girls. Once every five years we would go to Missouri for two or three weeks and in between Grandpa and Grandma Hershberger came to visit us. The first visit I have any recollection of was in 1935. All of the Hershberger siblings lived in the Garden City area except Uncle Elmer's and us. The first visit was also coordinated with Uncle Elmer's so we got to see those first cousins for the first time. My memory of the first visit is quite dim but I do remember that Grandma seemed very frail and had to have a special diet which looked better than what we were served. Grandpa was a kind and gracious man with a large flowing beard. He loved the outdoors and took us grandchildren on walks through the woods. He commented when he came to visit us in Tofield in 1932 he dug only two hills of potatoes for a full bucket but in 1937 in Mazeppa it took two rows to fill his bucket.

The second visit to Garden City which I remember much clearer was in the summer of 1940 during harvest. My grandparents lived with Uncle Raymond and Aunt Ida. I have to take my hat off to Aunt Ida who had something less

(Grandpa Hershberger family – Dad back row second from left – 1935)

than an ideal arrangement living with a demanding mother-in-law in her kitchen. She seemed to handle it graciously. Grandma was still on a special diet which apparently was helpful because she outlived Grandpa by a number of years! I thought it the better part of wisdom to give her a fairly wide berth because she seemed to believe that children needed to be seen but not heard. Since I didn't know what her problems were I shouldn't be too harsh with her but she was not a warm and fuzzy grandma who had lots of hugs and kisses. My mother would not have been able to do what Aunt Ida did so it is wonderful that she was never called upon to do it. I think Grandma thought my mother was something of a threat although I have no data to base it on.

Canada was at war with Germany when we visited in Missouri in 1940 and I was surprised at the lack of patriotism to the allied cause. I was also amazed at their criticism of President Roosevelt. Since we had a king in Canada who was completely off limits for criticism in our family, it seemed completely out of place to be criticizing your leader who had been elected by the people. Being a patriotic Canadian who believed in the divine right of the king, it was quite appalling.

My Hershberger uncles and cousins were not as large as their Brenneman counterparts but I was completely bowled over by the amount of ice cream they could put away. Ice cream in Canada was a dessert—in Missouri it seemed like a way of life. Five-gallon freezers of ice cream just evaporated. I enjoyed my Hershberger cousins since there were more of them my age than was true on the Brenneman side. The Hershberger gang enjoyed singing, which was special. Years later, at Hesston College, I sang with my cousin Earl Greaser in a male quartet. There were not many of my Brenneman first cousin males who really enjoyed singing.

I got exposed to molasses in Missouri and I remember the processing of the sorghum for the making of the same. Spending so much time and effort as they did on a marginal product did not seem very worthwhile. I enjoyed cooked mush, something we never had in Alberta, and scrapple which they ate with the molasses. It would have been tolerable with Rogers Corn Syrup. The cooking in Missouri was not as interesting to me as what I was served in Alberta but for a three week stint I was able to handle it. They also served sourdough bread with a starter that had started too long ago and instead of tasting sour it tasted rancid to me. That depended a bit on which aunt we visited, however. Aunts will go unnamed.

In looking back, I know I spent much more time with the Brenneman side of the family but I still came away with a deep respect for both families. The Hershberger family didn't have nearly as many chiefs as the Brenneman family but they both lived productive and useful lives. Two of my father's brothers were ordained ministers. Grandpa Hershberger had a modest farm that he owned; I'm sure it was debt free, but he did not think it was important to add field to field. He was more relaxed than Grandpa Brenneman but both of them treated me like I was someone they loved and appreciated. I probably was too harsh on Grandma Hershberger—I never walked in her shoes so I don't know what baggage she needed to carry. She did manage to raise a good and productive family. Grandma Brenneman was not a warm and fuzzy grandma either but she was much more approachable and I felt that she genuinely liked me. The Lord knows she fed me lots of meals.

After we moved to Kansas we got to see more of our Missouri family and interacted with them much more frequently.

The Mazeppa Years (1935-41)

I tend to use Mazeppa and High River interchangeably in the text because Mazeppa was our mailing address and High River was a town of 2,000 that was the focal point of the area that included Mazeppa. It was an economically depressed area, at the time, 200 miles south of Tofield.

We arrived in the town of Mazeppa at the Urias B. Gingrich residence the evening of November 27 and stayed with them overnight. Urias figured largely in our years at Mazeppa. He was a relatively prosperous farmer, trucker, repair shop, service station and threshing outfit operator. He and his wife Alice had a large family with whom we socialized quite often. He also provided employment for both of my parents at various times. Most of their children were girls with a boy, Gerald, with Downs syndrome, and Ed, who was just older than me. At the time we came Ed was in a children's hospital in Calgary for treatment of osteomyelitis, which they called TB of the bone. He came home from the hospital the following year and was back in school one grade ahead of me. We became good friends. He had to use crutches but was very agile.

There are only snippets of information that I remember from the first few days. Our home was four miles from Mazeppa, less than a quarter of a mile from the Bishop Isaac

(Our home in Mazeppa – 1935-41)

Miller residence and five miles from church. The property we rented was owned by a Mr. McKay who lived in Calgary and who rarely visited his property. We had a good set of buildings. The house, particularly, was a very nice two-story structure with a full basement and attic with central heating with a coal furnace. It was actually a better house than the one we left in Tofield so it did make that part of the transition easier for my mother. Because the water table was very high and there were artesian wells in the area, the basement would sometimes flood. We built a wooden platform at one end of the basement to have some area that was not under water if we had a heavy rain.

Our goods had been shipped from Tofield by freight car; one freight car had our furniture and equipment and one our livestock. Maurice Eby, a florid-faced rotund man weighing in at about 275 pounds, and Menno Guengerich, an older gentleman with craggy visage, helped move our belongings to our farm. This transport was primarily by wagon. The farm had an artesian well about fifty feet from the house. The developers of the farm had driven a casing into the well so the flow came out of a one-inch pipe. The water was very cold and was drained into a pond about a hundred yards east of our house. The water was heavily alkaline and had a distinct odor of sulfur. My father built a platform around the pipe so that you could stand on the platform to fill a bucket of water. Under the platform he installed hooks for hanging items needing refrigeration. At one time, before our arrival, they had tried to pipe the water into the house but it was abandoned because of lack of pressure of the artesian flow. Although the water had a somewhat unpleasant taste it was cold and plentiful. The pond below the house provided a good skating surface during the winter.

Since we moved during the school year we were immediately introduced into the school system and became acquainted with our teacher, Alsora L. Brown. I am not sure where her home base was but she lived in the small cottage owned by the school district just across the road from the school. The school was just a quarter mile from our house so we quite often came home for lunch.

I was in the third grade when we moved and she was my teacher for the remainder of that year plus the next full year. There were about twenty-five students in the school and included nine grades. Again there were a couple older boys that were basically in charge of at least the agenda for the male students. During the spring thaw we would go out into the pasture adjoining our school across the road and would drown out gophers and collect the tails. Since the gophers were a pest the provincial government paid a bounty of one cent for each tail collected. I am not sure that my mother appreciated the wet tails that needed to be rescued from my jeans. I don't think we ever redeemed the tails but we certainly collected them. We would go out into the field during the noon hour and happily pursue our quarry without thought of the time. Miss Brown would send one of the girls out into the field with the school bell and although we saw her coming with the bell we couldn't hear it so it could be honestly said that we had not heard the bell. I think, because I was one of the younger boys I did not get disciplined but the older boys had to write on the board *I will not be late for school again* a certain number of times. This is where the negotiation began. The teacher would start with fifty times but they would say "Please, Miss Brown, that's way too many" and she would start negotiating down. I think ten or fifteen times became the usual punishment. They apparently didn't know what they wrote because this was repeated many times. I don't think Glenn ever participated in that frolic.

She would read to us and enjoyed Zane Grey westerns so this was regular fare. It was probably not age appropriate but I enjoyed them with the bad guys always getting their just deserts in due time. Again the older boys liked being read to better than their school work and they would call, "Pleeease, Miss Brown, read some more." She usually did. It was seldom they didn't ask for more.

One time there was a measles epidemic going through the community and Miss Brown was behind a chalk board applying makeup to cover a quite bright rash. The older boys informed her that she had measles and would not be able to cover them with makeup. She did have the measles and we had a substitute teacher for a couple weeks.

We had an artesian well at school also and a nice pond suitable for skating on during the winter. We had some wonderful hockey games on that pond during the winter months. According to the *Pleasant Plains Proclaimer*, the school paper that was published during the tenure of our next teacher, Ivor Boon, I would want to go out and play hockey if it was warmer than thirty degrees below zero. I must have been very hard up to play hockey!

Mr. Boon was just out of teacher training and this was his first school. He instituted a monthly publication called *Pleasant Plains Proclaimer*. Pearl still has some of those papers which were produced by a process called hectograph. She has not been able to locate them but they really were very well done for a small school. Mr. Boon's sister was a columnist for the *Calgary Herald* and could have supplied some creative input. Glenn was the first editor of the above-mentioned paper, Pearl the second and your humble servant the third. I was also the first president of the *Pleasant Plains Carrot Growers Association*. This was a victory garden that we had in the school yard. He was by far the best teacher I had in grade school.

Mr. Boon was from Calgary but boarded at our place during the school week. He usually drove his model A Ford home to Calgary for the weekends. He would attend church with us when he stayed for the weekend. He was twenty-three years old when he began teaching me in the fifth grade and was my teacher for three years. He was tremendously innovative and made school a wonderfully fun experience. I got to see him twice as an adult while back to Alberta on a visit. The second time Martha was with me. He was retired from a school superintendent position in Calgary by that time. After meeting him Martha knew he had been a very unusual teacher. He had a passion for one-room schools and instituted a system in the Calgary schools of setting up a one-room school and rotating all of the students so they could spend one week during their grade school years in a one-room school with all of the grades. In his retirement he had gone all over Alberta finding and photographing all of the one-room schools still in existence. The Pleasant Plains School was now a feed lot so he had taken a picture of the cattle and titled it *The Class of 1995*, the year he took the picture.

He was a strict disciplinarian. Having been forewarned he laid down the law the first day of school. He was not without his faults. He decided fairly early which students were part of the problem and which ones part of the solution. He particularly picked on the Brietzke family, it seemed to me. Pat, a boy my age, was a handful but Mr. Boon never left any doubt as to who was in charge. Mr. Boon tended to put the Brietzke and the Guengerich children in the same pool when doling out his punishments. Pat's mother was a Guengerich but Pat's aunts, who were not problem children, were also in grade school with him. Pat's father had long since departed the scene but Pat with his brother Alex and sister Rosie lived with their mother at his grandparents' residence.

Much good could be said for the one-room school if you had a good teacher. I guess the same could be said for any class room. I enjoyed tuning in to other classes when they were having their recitations. History, geography and math were particularly fascinating to me. I enjoyed learning about what was going to be taught in future years. I wasn't particularly interested in the recitation of the lower grades except keeping an eye out for little brother John. James made his way without many ripples but John enjoyed mixing it up. The first grade had automobiles that progressed around the school wall to show their progress in reading. John's car was always far in the rear and the part that amazed me was he seemed to enjoy it back there. He was an unabashed teacher's pet. A rule at our house was that if we received a whipping at school (which we never did) we would receive one at home. Mr. Boon was aware of the rule and he told my parents one evening that John had deserved a whipping but didn't deserve two so he got by without one. Many years later John did very well in school but he never lost his charm!

John was the only one that Mr. Boon invited into his room at our home. One time when he was visiting in his room, Mr. Boon was studying and heard the sound of something falling. Upon inquiry John replied, "Oh, nothing much, I just dropped your watch!" Fortunately the watch was not broken. Mr. Boon recounted the incident to our mother and thought it was funny. Mother didn't think so. Another time mother served canned Bing cherries for dessert. Mr. Boon was enjoying them and when he went to his room Pearl counted twenty-eight cherry pits on his plate. The next day John reported to Mr. Boon what Pearl had observed. Neither John nor Mr. Boon was embarrassed but Pearl was. Commemorating that event, when Martha and I get Bing cherries we give twenty-eight of them to Pearl.

During this time the war was raging in Europe and we had a large map on the wall where the progress of the war was depicted graphically. We had a regular update on the current events of the world. Since we did not have a radio or a daily paper at home, these updates kept us somewhat informed on the events of the larger world.

Our next teacher was a Mr. Anderson and he was completely run over by the students. We had a large pot-bellied stove in the corner of the school and one day when Mr. Anderson was trying to discipline Pat Brietzke, standing by the stove, Pat took him down and sat on him. I was appalled since I had been taught you always respected and obeyed the authorities even when you didn't agree with them. During his time we decided to dig a cave in the school yard just southwest of the school entrance. The ground was a sandy loam so digging was not too difficult.

We dug a tunnel to the main room and put a chimney to let air, or smoke, out if we decided we would light a fire. We had enough room for about three or four boys to be in the room at one time. We made an escape tunnel out the back side. The top of the roof was about two or three feet under the surface of the ground. I don't know what our clothes looked like from all of the digging. The school board closed the project down very shortly after its completion and we got the opportunity to fill it back up. Mr. Anderson just lasted one year, my eighth grade.

Our next teacher was Milton Pritchard. He was a young married man who lived in the little cottage on the school grounds. I had him for only a few months of my ninth grade since we moved to Kansas in November. An expression that survived with our family, however, was a quote from Mrs. Pritchard. When they came to the community the school patrons had a surprise grocery shower for them. When we arrived Mr. Pritchard opened the door with his wife right behind him. They had not been expecting company and she exclaimed, "Oh, Milt, my hair!" I don't remember what her hair looked like but I remember the expression.

A major trauma of the Mazeppa years were the health issues for my brother Glenn. In the spring of 1937 Glenn got rheumatic fever. He was hospitalized for a short time but seemed to recover quite well. The next spring he got rheumatic fever again and, as I recall, was hospitalized for fifty-one days in the High River hospital. High River was fourteen miles from our place on dirt roads so we only went to see him about once a week. It was touch and go as to whether he would survive or not.

After he returned home my parents took him to a specialist in Calgary. He examined him thoroughly and then took my parents aside and told them he could not survive a year and probably less. On the way home Glenn asked them what the doctor had told them and so they told their sixteen-year-old son the opinion of the specialist. Coinciding with this event was the visit of T. K. Hershey, a long-term missionary from Argentina, who was holding meetings at our church. Glenn was always mature beyond his years and in consultation with my parents and T. K. Hershey he requested anointing. About a month later they returned to the specialist and after looking at the results of his prior visit he didn't believe this was the same person. They, of course, told him about the anointing. He acknowledged that he had no explanation for the change other than a miracle. Glenn's ill health and his upbeat attitude, even though facing a very uncertain tenure on earth, had a profound effect on me. I became very attached to my brother and it gave me a feeling of importance as the next oldest male, I had a special responsibility to step up and be counted.

It was during Glenn's long stay in the hospital that I committed a major indiscretion. After school one evening, against my better judgment, I went with several of the older boys to a swimming hole about four miles from school. I did not enjoy the swim because I knew I should be home and would not have received permission if I had asked. When I returned home the chores were already done and the family was waiting for me because they had decided to go visit Glenn in the hospital that evening. I was given two alternatives, receive a whipping, or stay home, while they went to High River. I really knew I needed a whipping for what I had done so it was the option I chose. I believe it was the last one I ever received.

Glenn, although much better, had irreversible heart damage. Although he looked healthy and carried on in a fairly normal manner he did have serious limitations in terms of hard physical labor so I was called upon to do much of the heavy lifting. Whereas my sister looked upon the Mazeppa years as the *Care Free Years* in her story of growing up it was the *Work Years* for me. The move from Tofield to Mazeppa on my ninth birthday was my initiation into the work force. I was up at the crack of dawn to help with the milking and other farm chores. My father was gone to Winter Bible School a week at a time, quite often, and during my eighth grade year my brother was at Hesston and my sister was in Winter Bible School also for several three-week stints and I was in charge of the farm chores. My sister and mother both helped with the milking when Dad was gone.

I had severe flu on several different times during the first two winters we were at Mazeppa and Dr. Burke decided that I should have my tonsils removed. The anesthesia that was used was ether. I remember the taste, smell and dizzy spiral as I went under the spell of the ether. This operation was in the early summer and that fall my father and I "stooked" our entire crop by ourselves. The approximately 200 acres was cut with a binder and we put all of the bound sheaves into what the Canadians called "stooks" and which the U. S. calls "shocks." During that summer when I became very tired the ether would revisit me with a very unpleasant taste in my mouth. I remember when we completed the job my father threw his hat up in the air and shouted "We did it!" I followed suit. I had worked with him every "stook" of the way.

In 1936 we had a complete crop failure so the family all went up to Tofield to help with the harvest there. Pearl and I attended the Solberg

School which was directly across the section from Grandpa's house. All of that ground was Grandpa's so we cut across the field. I was an outsider so was not particularly well received although some of the boys were ones that I had attended church with a year earlier. I think we were there for a little over a month and when we left they shipped a freight car load of straw to Mazeppa to help our cattle through the winter. It was at the Solberg School at the ripe age of nine I met my first heart throb, Wyonne Rudd. I never saw her again, after that month. Because we were involved in school I did not participate very much in the harvesting operation. I apparently had outgrown the need.

As a ten-year-old boy, I have a vivid memory etched on the retina of standing by the open grave of our neighbor and special friend of my mother who died of quinsy shortly after we moved to Mazeppa. Leona Hoover had come from Ontario and had married Maurice Eby. They had adopted a couple children and then had one together. She became ill quite suddenly and died. Her father, Mr. Hoover, a stranger to me, had come from Ontario for the funeral and he was standing on the north side of the grave and I was on the south side. He looked incredibly sad. One of the songs sung at her funeral was "Some day the silver cord will break." It touched my ten-year-old heart in a very unique way.

When we lived in Tofield we lived quite comfortably but we definitely felt the pinch of poverty in Mazeppa. The second year we again had a very short crop but we did have enough to go through the harvesting process. The second year Mother and Dad both worked on the U. B. Gingrich threshing crew. Mother managed the cook car and Dad was the flunky, which meant doing everything that was not otherwise assigned. They would leave at four o'clock Monday morning and return late on Saturday. There was a cook car where the cooking took place and a bunk car where the men slept. There was one long table running down the center of the cook car with a stove at one end. My parents slept on a pull-down cot. It was primitive. One morning before school I went with them because there was a sick horse that needed to be brought back. They were threshing about ten miles from where we lived so I went with them and after a hasty breakfast at the cook car drove the team with a wagon back to U. B. Gingrich's mother's home which was a mile from our place. I was having a very difficult time to get the sick horse to keep moving and finally about a mile short of our destination the sick horse lay down and died. I unhitched the other horse and led it to Mrs. Gingrich's home and told her that there was a dead horse about a mile north of her place that needed to be taken care of. I walked the mile home, picked up my lunch box, and went back to school. All in an eleven-year-old boy's work day!

We had a couple different young women who worked for us when my mother was working in the cook car. One was Marjorie Snyder, the adopted daughter of our neighbor, Isaac Miller, and another was Ermina Gingrich, the daughter of Emma Gingrich, a neighbor one mile from our place. They worked with Pearl to see that the house work was done and that the boys had clothes to wear and food to eat. For two years Glenn was well enough to help as a flunky on the threshing rig. When Glenn was at home, although he had to do only light duty, he was very important in keeping the ship upright. He was a young man mature beyond his years. We had a member at church, Gordon Good, who enjoyed kidding Glenn. One evening at church on a warm, quiet summer evening he greeted Glenn and Glenn responded, "The atmospheric pressure *is* a little oppressive to the respiratory organs." Gordon had a strange look, shook his head and walked away. Glenn didn't engage in athletic activities even before his bout with rheumatic fever. After his death an autopsy revealed an opening between the two upper chambers of his heart which would have been an impediment to vigorous activity.

My mother earned the handsome sum of four dollars per day. Mother always liked nice dishes and one year, after completing her work for the season she purchased a nice set of dishes with twelve place settings. These dishes stayed in the box, however, while she wrestled with herself about whether she should keep them or not when there were other pressing family needs. She eventually unpacked them and they became a much used set of dishes in our home. Each of us received a few pieces of the set but Glenna inherited a set of five when my mother died. She put them up for a fund raising auction at the Hershberger reunion in Oregon in 1996 and we purchased a set of four place settings.

In 1940 Urias bought a new pull type twenty-four foot John Deere combine. My father was asked to operate it. Combines were a new concept for our part of the country at that time. To open the field you had to run over the grain on the first round. I thought it would really be neat if the header was out in front so the grain wouldn't be run over and some of it wasted. I should have gotten a patent on the idea! Urias had also purchased two new Diamond T trucks. They were combining a field just south of Mazeppa and Urias asked me to take one of the trucks and get a load of grain and take it to the elevator in Mazeppa. I was all of thirteen years old, had driven the car a little but had never driven a big truck. It was the chance of a life time! I drove the truck to the field and had it fully loaded to head back to the elevator less than a mile away. The problem was the mile was fraught with peril. The roadways were graded very high with deep ditches on either side. Coming out of the field was a narrow approach and culvert leading onto a high road. I didn't have it in "grandma low" and stalled on the approach. The truck rolled back a short distance and I gave it another try, this time in the lowest gear. This time I realized I had not turned soon enough and I was going to go into the far ditch if I continued. I backed up again but this time I backed off of the culvert and I was stuck big time and the grain was pouring out into the ditch. What did Urias do? He got a hired hand to unload the truck into another truck and told me to get the other Diamond T and get the next load. This time I made a successful run. He never asked me to drive his truck again. Of course I didn't have a driving license either.

We moved to High River to serve the church there so the area deserves some attention. This community was almost all composed of persons who had come west from Ontario to seek their fortunes rather than from the United States. There were substantial cultural differences but we all spoke the same language, just with a different accent. The church in rural High River was a small group of believers with an attendance of about fifty to seventy persons. Most of the persons attending were ethnic German Mennonites. When we came my parents were actively inviting others to attend. Because of the dress and cultural differences many were not attracted but the Sunday school was active and those who felt they wanted their children to at least get a basic Christian education let their children attend. A large family living just one mile north of us, the Bert Rowland's, was one of those families. Mrs. Rowland brought her children to church. She was a believer and actively participated in the life of the church during the years we were there. They never became members, however. There were others although the church did not grow significantly while we were there. One of my memories was of an old gentleman, Elias Bricker, who lived in Calgary and was occasionally brought to church by his daughter. Because he was very hard of hearing he would sit beside the pulpit facing the audience and during sharing time he would intone "I believe the Lord is going to come VERY soon." That was an important reminder to all of us.

When T. K. Hershey, mentioned earlier in connection with the anointing service, was holding meetings, he stayed at our place. I had a high jumping standard out in the back yard that I would use and he came out to high jump with me. He was a rotund gentleman who measured all of five foot six inches and couldn't jump. I appreciated him coming out just the same. When we were going back to the house for supper he asked me whether I wanted to profess my faith in Christ that night. I said I did. It was a very releasing and freeing time for me because even though I was just a boy I had a plate full of responsibilities. It was the beginning of a life-changing walk. I was later baptized at the Mt. View Mennonite Church.

The Mt. View church derived its name from the spectacular view of the Canadian Rockies from our community. It was local lore that you could see the longest view of a mountain range at this location than anywhere in the world. In spite of the spectacular view, and the mountains only eighty miles away, it was not until we came back to visit years later we actually drove to those mountains.

Our next door neighbors, Isaac and Lydia Miller, were very special persons in our lives. They had two grown children, Fred who lived close by and farmed with his father, and Myrtle, a maiden lady who was working in Portland, Oregon at a mission home. Fred was married and had a family but did not attend church. One day he and his father were out spreading grasshopper poison on their crops. Fred was driving the tractor and Isaac was out on the trailer they were pulling throwing the poison out to the wind. When Fred was asked why he wasn't in the back and his elderly father wasn't driving the tractor, he replied, "Always wear the old machinery out first." I wasn't impressed with the reply but I always remembered it. Both Isaac and Lydia were what I would describe as "quaint." They had some mannerisms that were a bit unusual. Isaac had a unique way of burping that would sound like ZZZZZZZZT. He also had a unique way of clearing his throat followed with a couple short coughs. Many years later when I returned to Alberta with a men's quartet Isaac met us at the gate and did his throat clearing routine before he kissed me. Then he said "I presume all of these men are brethren" and then proceeded to kiss them as well. Lydia liked to entertain and also be entertained. They would occasionally invite themselves to Sunday dinner to one of their parishioners without prior warning. They did this once to the Menno Guengerich family. Mrs. Guengerich never attended church but when they appeared at their door one Sunday noon Mrs. Guengerich said, "Sometimes it suits, and sometimes it doesn't suit, today it doesn't suit." The Millers returned home.

Because the ground was very alkaline around our house because of the artesian well, we had our garden plot at the Miller place. We built a stile to get over the fence into the garden plot which was close to the road— their house was set back a couple hundred yards. Mrs. Miller would sometimes invite us over for "leavings" or food that had been left over from a prior meal. Mrs. Miller always fussed about how good the food was. It was OK by my standards but I didn't think it was appropriate to brag about it.

Life was not all work and duty. We would quite often go on picnics and sometimes combined picnics with work. A fruit that grew wild and native to that part of Alberta were June berries, which were called saskatoons. The bushes grew along the river banks and one of the annual events was going up to the Bow River, about nine miles north of our place and pick saskatoons. We would pack a picnic lunch and eat it beside the clear rushing mountain stream. We would also wade in the river but it was uncomfortably cold. We would take our berries home and Mother would can them, quite often with rhubarb because the berries were quite bland and needed the tartness to jazz them up. The Urias Gingrich family would sometimes accompany us on that excursion.

We also would picnic at the Prince Edward Island Park which was an island formed by the Bow river. There was a large dinosaur that was constructed in 1937 that was rather spectacular. Martha and I saw it when we went back to Alberta in 2010. The park contains a very nice zoo now. High River also had a good park and the church would use this as a place to eat, play and socialize.

When our parents went to Calgary during the week when we were in school, we would wait for them to come home. Pearl would prepare the meal and we would stand at the west window of our kitchen to see when they would come. The main highway from Calgary to High River was nine miles west of our place but we could see the lights of any car turning off the highway coming our way. We would try to guess if it was them by the speed and the intensity of the lights. It usually was them because there was very little traffic on our road. When we children went with them, we would sometimes eat at the Maple Leaf Café, a Chinese restaurant in downtown Calgary where you could get a three-course meal for twenty-five cents.

Ivor Boon's sister, a columnist for the *Calgary Herald* wrote an article about the cheapest and most expensive eating places in Calgary. The most expensive meal was at the Palliser Hotel, $3.50 and the cheapest at the Palace Café for fifteen cents. A good wage for a day's work was three dollars at that time. We, of course never ate at the Palliser although on a return visit Martha and I tasted their cuisine. It was tasty and served in style.

A phenomenon of the area was mirages. We could see the elevators of Mazeppa and sometimes they would be doubled and occasionally the image would be inverted, one on top of the other.

Chinook winds were also a unique feature. When there was an arch of clear sky over the Rockies on a cloudy day it was a good chance that a warm wind would arrive. It could be twenty degrees below zero and we would wake up with the eaves dripping water. Even though we had a tight house when we had a blizzard there would be snow on top of the blankets needing to be shaken off when we jumped out of bed.

When my father came up the steps at night he would be munching on a cracker and winding the alarm clock. It was a nighttime ritual that made me feel secure. Sometimes when he had been gone for a time he would let me "sleep in" and would not wake me to help with the chores. I would hear him getting ready and when I heard him go by my door and go down the stairs I knew I had a reprieve from the chores that morning. I would snuggle in and thank the Lord.

Although my father was neither eloquent nor trained he was a vigorous student and spent a lot of time on preparing sermons. He did not have the time to read to us like he did in Tofield so my younger brothers missed out on what the three oldest received. He was well respected in the community and he was helpful in bringing new persons into the church. His piety did not allow for participation in community secular activities. Ivor Boon had him teach music to the students since Ivor was tone deaf. Dad did the training but would not participate in the school programs. Ivor wondered aloud about that when we met him in Calgary in 1996. I really didn't have a good answer for him.

We did not have indoor plumbing but in the winter we would have a commode in the basement that was vented into the chimney for doing our daily constitutional. Carrying the pail out was never part of my duty. During most of the year, even when it was still cold, we would use the outhouse. The paper for cleaning up was an out-of-date catalog from

Hudson Bay or The Eaton Company. This was one case where I preferred the black and white pages to the colored ones on glossy paper!

A good source of income for me was trapping weasels in the fifty days before Christmas. Glenn started the business but I took over after he became ill. We set traps about a quarter mile apart. This usually was along a fence row. We would place the bait, a piece of meat or fat, on the barbed wire above the trap. When the weasel jumped for the bait it landed in the trap. The trap line was about five to seven miles long and I would service it every other day during the period before Christmas. I would ride the line with my horse and would put the weasels in my saddle bag. The weasels were usually frozen to death but sometimes they would still be alive. They had a powerful scent bag, at least as powerful as a skunk, so great care needed to be exercised in approaching them. Their scent bag was usually almost empty because they had expended their store by the time I got to them. Because I was trapping them for the fur it could not be damaged without penalty. When I had the weasel pinned down I would grab it and choke it to death. One time, after completing this ritual, I put the weasel in my bag only to discover it had come back to life. Fortunately it was still groggy so I was able to complete the task. After I got home with my catch, usually two or three, I would skin them in the basement, mount them on a board, inside out, and let the pelt dry. During the summer the weasel looks very much like a prairie gopher, in terms of color but when cold weather comes it turns snow white except the end of the tail which was jet black. The fur is almost worthless until it is completely white. The weasels seem to disappear after Christmas so we discontinued trapping after Christmas. I would get about thirty weasel pelts per season and they would be worth from seventy cents to $1.50 for a premium pelt. This provided a very nice cache for purchasing needed clothing. It was never used for fun and games but was used to purchase gifts for other members of the family. Since winter wages were not more than two dollars per day it was a nice bundle. Later on in life I thought of

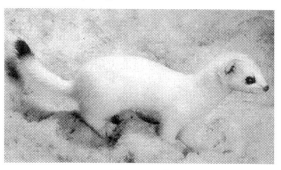

(the weasel)

buying Martha an ermine coat but didn't because we never went any place where she could wear it!!

There were no potatoes grown in the Mazeppa area in 1937 so my father, with Urias Gingrich decided to go to Duchess, an irrigated community, to purchase a truck load of potatoes. It was cold, I'm not sure how cold, but it definitely was freezing. The wisdom they subscribed to was that if you kept moving the potatoes would not freeze. They kept moving and upon arriving at our place put the whole load of potatoes into our basement. Persons in the community knew about the enterprise so they came to our place to purchase potatoes in hundred pound bags. Although they had kept moving the potatoes froze and there arose a great stench from the basement. Fortunately they were able to salvage some but most of the potatoes were fed to the pigs.

Another money-raising scheme was the "butchering ring." This consisted of a weekly butchering at Emma Gingrich's, one mile west of our place. Each week one of the farmers in the ring would donate a beef. It was butchered and by a pre-set formula each person would get a certain cut of meat. It worked well. It seems like there could be lots of ways in which this could have been cause for misunderstandings and bickering but it continued for several years during the winter months. My father was in charge of the slaughtering and I'm sure Urias Gingrich was involved at some level.

In 1939 we had a Men's Chorus from Hesston give a program at our church. There were only sixteen men in the choir but Uncle Paul, who had been a student at Hesston the prior year, came down to Mazeppa for the program. He was good friends with some of the choir members and they had a pretty noisy time at our home that night. Two of the choir members who stayed at our place were Jake Heatwole and Waldo Miller. I think there were some others but I can't remember their names.

I should mention my next heart throb. Even though I was still in grade school I knew the difference between boys and girls. Gloria Gage, a good friend of my sister Pearl was one that struck my fancy. She was an excellent skater and athlete with blond hair and a very prominent Roman nose. Gloria was a formidable foe with a hockey stick. She sometimes attended church with us even though her parents never did. Her father was manager of one of the grain elevators at Mazeppa and lived across the road from the elevator. Pearl thought her older brother Ralph was rather special, even though I didn't see anything special about him. Gloria was two grades ahead of me but that didn't keep me from admiring her.

Ermina Gingrich, a younger sister of Urias, lived a mile west of our place with her mother. Her father had died before we moved to Mazeppa. Ermina was a member of our church and rather early set her eyes on Glenn. She was a beautiful woman but a bit too worldly wise. She was a year or two older than Glenn and was already out of grade school when we moved

(Howard, Mom, James, Glenn, John, Dad, Pearl – 1938)

into the community. I was only peripherally aware of this attraction but mother was not unaware of the stirrings of interest. Although my mother did not usually involve herself in the romances of her children I definitely had the feeling that Ermina was not a favorite. Ivor Boon, our teacher, also had his eyes on her but she apparently did not have eyes for him.

I give this background because it fits into the larger picture for the future of our family. Mother had not been able to attend high school until she was seventeen years old, when they sent her to Hesston. She had a wonderful experience that was cut short, halfway through her first year, because her mother became ill and she was needed at home to take care of her siblings. Grandpa and Grandma Brenneman certainly could have hired a maid to take care of the family but I don't think they thought education was a high priority for a girl so she had to return home after the first semester. Getting the "Hesston experience" for her children became a very high priority for my mother. She also saw a limited field of potential mates for her children in the Mazeppa community. As mentioned earlier, we went to Missouri to visit in the summer of 1940. We returned from this trip through Hesston where Uncle Charlie and Aunt Pearl Greaser lived. After visiting with the administration of Hesston College, they decided to leave Glenn in Hesston with the Greasers. He attended

Hesston the following school year. It was somewhat traumatic to leave Glenn in Hesston for my parents and for his siblings. Even though he was limited in what he could do physically he was a mental and spiritual source of strength to the whole family. He had taken high school work by correspondence with the help of Mr. Boon so he entered Hesston as a high school senior. He wrote regularly and we thoroughly read his letters. He reported, after going to hear the Messiah performance in Lindsborg, they sang Amen for seven pages. Not being acquainted with this piece of music, I was impressed. We got the Lark publication that year and by the time we moved to Hesston I had the names of all the students memorized.

The winter of 1940 my sister Pearl got to go to Winter Bible School at several of the Alberta Mennonite Churches. The sessions lasted three weeks and were taught by ministers from different congregations. Principal teachers were Milo Stutzman, Ezra Stauffer and Clarence Ramer. My father would go to those sessions occasionally and teach as well as attend. Pearl was gone for nine weeks in total during the winter of 1940. Sessions rotated from church to church and she became good friends of some of the young people in the conference as a result. Cicely Rogers and Beulah Good became life-long friends of hers and they have stayed in touch ever since. Blizzards were common during the winter months. One time my father had been at Duchess at a church meeting and on the way home was caught in a blizzard. There were twenty persons marooned in a small shack for two days while help came to open the roads. In the shoveling out process one of the men, Abe Wideman, suffered a heart attack and died. Without telephone communication we had no idea what had become of them for a couple days. I have no memory of worrying about their safety but I'm sure my mother did.

At the Hesston College commencement in the spring of 1941 Urias and Alice Gingrich took my parents with them to the graduation ceremonies. I think that event sealed the decision—we were going to move to Hesston. There was no way us children would be able to attend Hesston unless we moved.

In September of 1941 my Grandpa Hershberger died but we were unable to attend the funeral. We had seen him in the summer of 1940—I liked him a lot. He was a kind, gentle, and loving man.

That fall, just a few days before Pearl Harbor, we had a sale and moved to Hesston. Father got an old running gear and built a box on it for the homemade trailer that we used to take our possessions to Kansas. We were pulling it with a 1931 Chevrolet. School was having recess when we went by and I was ashamed enough of our rig that I

(Ready to roll to Hesston – Pearl, Howard, Dad and James-1941)

slumped down in the seat so I wouldn't be seen by my fellow classmates. I'm not sure why it was necessary to hide! We left Alberta with a little cash, a small trailer load of possessions, a $1000 Canadian government bond and a lifetime of experience. To give you a little perspective, a new auto could be purchased for less than $1000 but we did not bring any major furniture with us.

When we got to the US border they were examining our group with some vigor and to see that our documentation was in line. My parents did not have a birth certificate or even proof of birth for me. The customs official said, "He looks like all the rest of them but without proof of birth he does not go." We then went back to the small village of Coutts, Alberta to wire to Edmonton for documentation. We spent the night on the border before the documentation came and we were able to proceed.

I left the Mazeppa years with some questions. Is there a different life than just working hard every day and barely eking out a living? Why does Brother Glenn have to be sick? How will I get along without hockey?

Musings on the Mazeppa years

The Mazeppa years were times of forced growth for me. I went to Mazeppa, a kid with a lot of questions. I left with some directions in mind. Financially we came to Mazeppa rather middle class—we left financially poor. My parents never had a bank account during the years we lived in Mazeppa. We lived hand to mouth. The produce we raised was sold for cash money. I'm not sure if Grandpa Brenneman helped financially during this time or not. I rather suspect that he did not. He was a free enterprise believer and you sank or swam on your own.

I am rather amazed, looking back, at the rigor of my work schedule as a pre-teen and an early teenager. It was expected of me to take responsibility and I did. There was no feeling sorry for myself or thinking that life was unfair, or someone else should be doing this. I sometimes felt guilty when I spent time playing rather than finding work to do even though I never was chided by my parents when I took time out to play. I felt very much loved and appreciated by my parents. They recognized with appreciation my contribution to the family. That seemed enough for me. I was not a social person like either Glenn or Pearl. I would spend lots of time by myself. A favorite time was going after the cows, over a mile walk away, usually. I had a lot of conversations out loud with just me, the sky, the pasture, and the cows.

Our poverty was a source of tension in the family. During the dust bowl years, when it was so dark the chickens would go to roost in the middle of the day, I would lie on the sofa, cover myself over the head and go to sleep—it was my way of avoiding reality. Living in poverty was something I was going to try very hard to avoid. That was partly responsible for my decision to become a doctor as three of my uncles had done.

James and John were still kids finding their way. James was enough younger than me that he didn't get very involved in farm labor during our time in Mazeppa. John enjoyed hanging out with the women and they enjoyed having him around. James and John usually did things together. John was the chief instigator of chicanery, and James, being the older of the two usually got the blame. At their age they were largely unaware of our poverty.

I developed a love for the church during these difficult times and I would spend time while working in the field singing and meditating. I didn't drive the tractor very often but usually worked the ground with a six-horse hitch. Solitude was something to be cultivated and appreciated.

I did not develop any lifelong close friendships while at Mazeppa. I am not sure of the reason—perhaps I was too young or perhaps I was too introverted. Close friendships were developed within the small church community and I was really limited to the small community of Mazeppa during those years. Pearl and Glenn had opportunities in the larger church family in Alberta when I was too young to participate.

Father never played team sports with us. I don't remember him ever skating or swinging a bat or playing catch. He took a dim view of organized sports. He did not attend ball or hockey games I participated in, frowning on my participation, but never forbidding it. Glenn did not participate in those events, girls didn't and James and John were too young, so I was the sole recipient of his concern. It was not a major issue between us but it was there. After we moved to Kansas this was not a problem since the participation was only intramural.

Mother did not seem to feel well a lot of the time when we lived in the Mazeppa community. I think there was a good deal of worry about what would happen to them and their family. Christian education and life mates were front and center in her concerns. This became more important as we children grew older. She had to find a way for us to leave Mazeppa. Dad, although supportive, was more willing to go with the flow. Mother needed to create the flow.

The Hesston Academy Years (1941-46)

Our trip to Hesston was uneventful except for a wheel bearing that went out on the trailer so we needed to stay in Shelby, Montana an extra day. We had a very nice motel so it was quite pleasurable. It had a small kitchen so mother cooked our meals. She always liked to stay in motels that had kitchen facilities and later, when they built their own motel, the amenities that were built in were the ones she thought were important when traveling.

We stayed at Uncle Charlie's the first night but I think we were very quickly ensconced in our own rented house on Main Street. The house was owned by Henry Pfautz and is the one currently owned by Marion Bontrager right across the street from the college. The rent was eighteen dollars per month. It was the first time we ever lived in town, had indoor plumbing, electricity and a telephone. What to do with all the time? I couldn't believe there was life without farm chores! My father fixed that quite soon by buying a cow that was tethered at Harry Kauffman's home two blocks away. It was closer to the edge of town and had a small barn. I didn't have to milk the cow every time although I think I got to do it oftener than anyone else. My father got a job at the local feed mill owned by Roy Troyer. He received the princely sum of seventeen dollars for a forty-five hour week. Uncle Charlie quickly caught on there were some potential farm hands needing work to do. Lawrence and Earl were integrated into the community into activities that kept them occupied so he would hire us to do various errands. Although I liked Uncle Charlie, he paid us the same he would have paid his own sons—next to nothing. Soon after coming to Hesston we traded the 1931 Chevrolet in for a dark blue 1938 Pontiac straight eight. It was a wonderful improvement and a very serviceable vehicle.

I immediately enrolled in the academy at Hesston. I was a freshman and Pearl was a sophomore—I had advanced one grade on her since she had been out of school a year. I remember receiving a couple *incomplete* grades the first term because I didn't realize there was work to be made up because of my late start. That was soon rectified and I was fully in the swing of school work. To have fifty classmates was a completely new experience. One of those was Martha Buckwalter whom I saw without seeing for a couple years. Another person was my first cousin, Earl Greaser, whom I sang with later when we were in college. To be in classes with such a large number of fellow believers was a distinctive experience.

When I enrolled I was asked what I was planning on doing as a life work. There were only two things I was aware you did—one was farming and the other was medicine. Of the two, medicine seemed more exciting so I chose medicine first and farming second. I hadn't really thought about it before being asked the question but it directed my course choices, particularly in college.

Music was of interest from the beginning and the first year I sang in the choir that everyone could participate in if they chose to. There were no competitive tryouts. At the beginning of my sophomore year I was in the choir that included high school and college individuals. I also sang in the men's choir. Although my voice range was baritone, I chose bass, hoping I would become one! During my junior year I was on the committee to select the singers. I came to the conclusion, based on a small sample, seventy-five percent of the men were baritone but some of them needed to sing second tenor and some of them *got* to sing bass. The rest could be baritone. An event transpired during the tryouts that bothered me for a long time. I told one of the persons trying out I was rooting for him to become a member when in fact I voted with those who felt he was not good enough. He was not selected but I repented of my duplicity for a long time. It did not seem appropriate to confess to him so where could I receive absolution when there was no priest? God knew my sorrow and finally gave me peace.

During the beginning of my junior year my father agreed to become the manager of the college farm. The Mennonite Board of Education had title to the college and was responsible for the farm that was a part of the college. At that time the farm consisted of only about eighty acres of farm and pasture land but a dairy of thirty to forty mixed-breed

(Howard, James, John & Jenny the mule)

milk cows. We also had pigs and chickens. The farm house was located where the Kropf Center is and the barn where the Yost Center is. We supplied raw milk for the college as well as the town. We had a delivery route for our milk we ran every day, Monday through Saturday. Jenny, the mule, was used to pull a two-wheeled cart. I was the main man for delivering milk. We would be up before five a.m. every morning to milk the cows and then load the cart with milk for the run. The milk was put into glass jars, either quart or gallon, and then returned for washing and refilling. When a customer wanted milk they put empty containers on their porch and we would leave them the same amount. Jenny knew the route by heart but when we had a change of course because of a new or different customer she would have to be re-programmed. It would take about three or four mornings to achieve this but then she would occasionally go back to the prior route so I had to be alert. I also discovered what some of our customers wore for night wear as well as when they got up in the morning. One morning, while it was still dark I was running across a yard with milk in hand and discovered a new clothesline. I learned what it was like to be literally "clotheslined." Delivering the milk in this manner was quite efficient because I stood on the back of the cart on a low step and could deliver the milk with Jenny never stopping. Later, when Jenny died, we delivered by pickup and it usually meant having a driver and a deliverer.

We purchased a milking machine system a year or two after we went to the college farm. A very memorable event was one evening I was left alone to milk the thirty-six head of cows and the electricity went off. I milked all of them by hand. As you might appreciate, they were at least relieved of their load if not fully milked! Shortly after completing the task the electricity came back on.

During the summers at the end of my freshman and sophomore years I worked at the Gaius Horst farm between Hesston and Newton. I stayed there all week

Dad and me in Wichita – 1944)

usually coming back on Saturday night and returning Sunday night after church. He had a medium-sized farm and a small dairy of registered Guernsey cows. I did general farm work and helped with the milking. The milk had to be refrigerated over at the Elmer Hershberger farm, a larger dairy, having refrigeration equipment. They had a number of children including a couple beautiful girls my age. Even though they were Mennonites they attended Newton High School. It was not too difficult to get me to go over to deliver the milk!

I learned what it was like to try to start a two cylinder JD tractor when I stalled it plowing. It was almost impossible to start. Rather than a crank, we used for our McCormick-Deering, it had a large flywheel that you spun to get it started. It was 100 degrees one summer day when I stalled it while plowing. I didn't have gloves and I blistered my hands rather badly before I got it started. I was a full member of the harvest crew for threshing and I got very tired and lost some weight during the summer of my freshman year. I also drank a lot of water to keep from being dehydrated which needed to be taken care of during the night. I woke up needing to urinate (they didn't have indoor plumbing) so I went downstairs only to discover the doors locked with a key from the inside and I didn't have a key. Rather than wake Gaius, I went back upstairs, opened the window and let it fly. My bedroom was right over the bedroom of my host family and at breakfast Maggie said, "I thought I heard it raining last night but I guess I was mistaken." I secured a receptacle to take to my room for any such emergencies in the future. I also was more careful of my liquid intake.

I was large for my age but I was not very muscular so I think I looked stronger than I was. Particularly when I was only fifteen the farm work tested my metal. I wasn't just acting like a man, as in Alberta, I *was* a man receiving a man's wages. On a couple occasions I got pitted against the neighbor Earl Horst, Gaius's nephew, who was a grown married man. One day we were loading sorghum bundles on to a wagon. They had not set the binder correctly and the bundles weighed close to 100 pounds each. We picked these up over our heads to load them on to the wagon to take to the forage chopper. I almost died struggling with them while he nonchalantly threw them on like they were feather pillows. Later I heard other stories about his strength, when he was past his prime, from sons John and Daniel who worked with him on bridge construction when they were starting to college. He was a modern "Samson."

Beginning with my junior year in high school we lived on the college farm so I had plenty of work to occupy my time during the school year. I was also on the baseball team and did very well that fall. When the winter season came, my classmates who were new that year were counting on me for the basketball team. I had never had a basketball in my hand until I came to Hesston and I never had any proficiency in the sport. It soon became obvious that I could not be counted on.

Martha had stayed out of school during her normal sophomore year so she "could learn to work." This was a program her mother had set up for her daughters. This was waived when the youngest sister, Esther Rose, went to high school. When she returned to school as a sophomore, I was a junior; I suddenly became aware of her. She had turned from a lanky adolescent to a charming teenager who glided when she walked and was a good athlete. I dated Elaine Yoder, a girl from Iowa, on occasion during my junior year, but I believe she was not overly impressed with me. During the summer after my junior year, I asked Martha for a date. The lilt in her voice when she said "yes" became a trademark. She expressed appreciation for all of the little kindnesses I showed that have continued throughout our years together. We had a date in December on which I was "bummed out" for no reason other than I was depressed. I didn't ask her again for a time. Elaine Yoder had not come back to school until the second semester

45

and I asked her for a date and took her to our church for a Sunday evening program. Martha had a topic that night that she presented and looking out into the congregation she saw me with Elaine. She later told me it was the worst night of her life. I had a couple more dates with Elaine and then realized it was a losing proposition so I went into a mild funk.

World War II was raging and gas was rationed and vehicles were in short supply on the campus. I had access to my parents' car and there were a couple fellows who wanted to have dates to the *Messiah* at Lindsborg so I agreed to take them. I was not dating anyone so I decided that I would ask the seventh girl to come out of chapel since seven is the perfect number. I asked this lady and she accepted. When I checked her out of the girl's dormitory, which was the custom, I couldn't remember her name. I had to ask her and the date went downhill from there. Meanwhile one of the guys I was taking had asked Martha and she was having a wonderful time in the back seat (four people in very close proximity to each other) while I was in splendid isolation in the front seat. Rachel Horst, a name I can never forget, was hugging the passenger side door post. We went up to Coronado Heights, the highest point in Kansas, after the concert and then home. The next week I asked Martha for a date and she had the same lilt in her voice as the first time I asked her. She said, "YES." (She didn't say it like that but it was the way it sounded to me.) The fellow that had the date with her, unnamed, was a bit peeved that she started going with me again and turned him down when he asked her. I refused to feel sorry for him! Martha and I continued dating from then on until our marriage several years later.

Our family quickly became integrated into the community. During the first year my father would accept preaching assignments in neighboring communities and there was some conversation about us living in another community than Hesston. When we worshiped in Hesston we attended the Pennsylvania Mennonite Church about three miles out in the country. Martha's father, Earl Buckwalter, was the sole pastor so the congregation was looking for someone to help in the ministry. Paul Erb, the prior minister, had taken a teaching assignment at Goshen College and had left the summer before we came to Hesston. My father was asked to preach on a couple occasions and then was asked to assume an assistant pastor role. I don't know if the congregation voted on it or not but we were very well accepted even though Dad did not have the qualifications of Paul Erb.

Our family did a lot of socializing and we children were always included. Dinners were at Chris Vogts, the Redigers, Irl Coopriders, Roy Troyers, Oliver Millers, Charlie Greasers, Harry Kauffmans, and Earl and Rose Buckwalters, mostly close neighbors. Of this group only the Buckwalters and Millers were members of the Pennsylvania Church. These persons were also guests in our home. Mother loved to entertain and it continued unabated during her entire lifetime! Sister Pearl picked up the entertainment mantra and continues the tradition.

Prayer meetings, held in the homes, were a regular event on Wednesday night. Our family always went. It usually consisted of about twenty-five to thirty persons, mostly adults. There was always a Bible study followed by a special prayer time. One night I decided I wasn't going to go; it had been cold and there was ice on the pond. I had been invited to a skating party by Clifford King on his Uncle Alvin's pond south of Burrton. My parents were not pleased but I argued that there so seldom is ice I didn't want to miss the chance. When we got to the cabin we discovered that it was on fire so we rushed over to Burrton to notify the fire department, most of whom were in the domino parlor. They came outside to look and you could see the blaze from five miles away. We went back and skated by the light of the fire and then roasted wieners on the dying embers. I think my parents took it as an opportunity to point out that bad things happen when you're running away from the Lord.

Since the college had daily chapel services as well as special meetings I attended a lot of church events. In addition to this I was taking Bible courses in the academy. There were a number of memorable chapel events. One that sticks out was one presented by Gerald B. Winrod. Two of his sons attended Hesston Academy. He was anti-war, pro-German and strongly anti-Semitic. He published a magazine called the *Defender* to propagate his beliefs. He lived in Wichita and he had a BIG voice and he started out his chapel with I KNOW THAT I KNOW THAT I KNOW THAT I KNOW THAT I KNOW. I don't remember what he KNEW but I remember his preamble. I always thought that he had been invited to come to chapel because of his boys but I understood later he had a strong following among the Mennonites and his monthly magazine was published by the *Herald Press* in Newton. I took typing with his son John who had a beater of a typewriter retired from their publishing business. It was a *very* noisy machine. On timed drills when the rest of the class was half way across the page you could hear the slam of his carriage return and the rat-a-tat-tat of his continued typing. He regularly typed well over 100 words a minute.

I did well enough in school but could have spent more time studying than I did. I was an early believer in the 80-20 rule. It took twenty percent of the time to get eighty percent of the material and from then on there were diminishing returns. I guess I often settled for that unless the material was of particular interest to me.

When I was due to begin my senior year I knew that I was going to be drafted if I stayed in school so I opted to try for a farm deferment. We had a large enough farming operation to justify it since we had acquired more farm land and had begun a hay baling business. We had purchased an International baler from Ivan Diller and ran it for one year and then had the opportunity to get a Case baler which was the state-of-the-art baler. It was the time of price controls but through Earl Berner we were able to locate a baler in North Dakota at retail price and a model A Farmall tractor. The total rig came to about $2400. We used it for two years and with price controls gone sold it for $3500 when we left the college farm. We made excellent money baling and it was all deposited into the common family treasury. The first job was baling a musty straw stack and I was handling the needles without a mask and got two lungs full of dust. I ended up in the hospital in Newton. Thanks to the introduction of penicillin I survived but I was climbing the walls in a delirium for a couple days. It was a lesson learned.

When I finished my junior year I became the point man for baling in the area and did it for two summers. I ran the needles, James tied and John drove the tractor. Between my father and me we lined up work. One of the first of a couple bad experiences was when we were having trouble with the pickup tines getting stuck. I was in front trying to get them in the groove and John was running the tractor, but not according to my liking. I shouted at him to get off and let James drive. John obliged and then went and sat on a board that we had mounted on the back of the feeder. He sat on the board, James backed up onto John's toe which pinned his leg and then proceeded to back up his leg. There was no place for his leg to go since he was sitting on the bench mounted to the baler. John received a bad break. To my discredit, I didn't think his leg was broken and told him to quit complaining. He soon convinced me it was for real and we took him to the doctor. We then were without a driver and had a lot of work lined up. We called on the relatives and got Derald Brenneman, Uncle

Titus's oldest son, to drive. He was younger than brother John and had never driven a tractor in his life so there was a serious learning curve. He tried and we eventually were operating close to normal again.

When we were operating the old International baler we had to use "blocks" to separate the bales. Occasionally they would get damaged when the plunger pushed them down before the hay cleared. I was rebuilding one of those blocks on the table saw that was set up in our house on South Main that was under construction. While using the table saw in the rebuilding process I almost completely severed my left thumb. I was immediately dispatched to Uncle Fred's office and he re-attached it and tried to tie the severed tendons back together with limited success. The joint of my left thumb does not function and my appendage protrudes like a sore thumb. The blood circulation was also impeded so it is usually cold. I was sharpening a stake later and cut off the corner of the index finger of my left hand. Years later I completed the massacre of my left hand by breaking three and dislocating all of my fingers in a nasty fall in Salina. (My left hand was also the one severely frozen earlier so the fingers are stubby.)

That summer Martha worked for my mother. She got some immersion in the ways of the Hershbergers. Since John had a cast on his leg he was able to provide the necessary guidance for Martha to learn the ways of our family!! They enjoyed each other and both survived. Martha took some good-natured jabs from friends about whether she was working for my family to earn my hand. Martha drove the pickup occasionally for the milk delivery and the monthly collection of the milk money from the customers. I didn't see her very often since she came after breakfast and left before supper.

I was registered as a conscientious objector to the war. The local draft board sent a letter to Milo Kauffman, the president of the college, to determine if my character justified the classification. By mistake, Milo's secretary sent the letter to me rather than the draft board.

(Martha, my love-1946)

49

After carefully reading it I forwarded it to the draft board. His evaluation of me was an important, if painful, experience. What he saw and what I thought I was were quite different. Although he recommended that I be granted the CO classification he saw me as aloof and watching things happen rather than working at constructive good. I have always been analytical and sometimes cynical so he might have had good cause for his evaluation but it was the first time I had a completely candid evaluation by someone who didn't know I was going to see it. I think it was helpful. I got the CO classification and a farm deferment.

By this time my Brenneman grandparents plus uncles Harvey, Fred, Joe, James, and Titus with their families had all moved to Hesston. On March 24, 1946, my Grandpa Brenneman died suddenly, from cerebral meningitis. I was unable to attend the funeral because I was quarantined for scarlet fever. His two doctor sons, one practicing in Hesston and one in Moundridge, were rather shocked by his sudden passing. Our Brenneman family didn't get together as often as they had in Alberta because they were in varying occupations and didn't have the bond of farming as in Alberta. I thought he was quite old but was only sixty-eight. He had a shock of white hair that added to his dignity. Since all of his family was present they took a family picture and inserted Grandpa into the picture. This was before the advent of digital photography so it was only partly successful. Grandma, sitting by the empty chair, looked terribly sad. In due time Harvey, Fred and James with their families all moved away and left only my parents and the Joe and Titus families in the community. After Grandpa died Grandma lived by herself for eight years and in her last year moved into my parents' home on South Main Street. At the reading of the will, all of the land in Alberta

(My parents home built in 1945 and Martha and my first upstairs apartment)

was left to the children while Grandma only received the two quarters that she had inherited from her parents but had been deeded over to my grandpa. She was left with other assets and never had financial need but the attorney visited her privately later, and asked if she wanted to contest the will since she was left with very little of the land. Fortunately she did not share this visit with my uncles until years later. If she had I'm sure they would have paid the attorney a visit and given him the what for!

In the spring of 1946 I went through the high school graduation exercises with the class that Martha was part of. I had taken enough credits by correspondence during the two years I was out of school, to complete my high school requirements. A class that I took from the University of Nebraska was English literature. I thoroughly enjoyed it. English teachers particularly embarrassed me with their fawning over the literature. I liked to read it my way. I still have the book that I used and refer to it occasionally although now I usually look up a poem I'm interested in on Google.

At the end of the summer of 1946 I was notified to appear for my physical exam for the draft since my farm deferment was going to be terminated. We sold our baler and tractor and my parents decided to move off the college farm. They realized that they were soon going to be running out of free labor! The week before I was to appear for my physical the draft was discontinued.

In 1945 my parents built a house on South Main in anticipation of leaving the college farm. This is the house that was directly in front of Schowalter Villa and was moved over to Ridge Road in Hesston. During the war it was very difficult to get building materials so my father found a house in Aulne, and tore it down for the material. Uncle Charlie helped with the demolition and was rather seriously injured when a wall fell on him and hit him in the face. Although the injury was not life-threatening his eye socket sagged the rest of his days. Grandpa Brenneman even helped by straightening out nails to be reused. When it was completed Uncle James's moved into the lower half of the house and the upper half was used for an auxiliary girls dormitory for one or two years.

A note that should be made about my high school years was my continuation of asocial behavior or as I would prefer to call it, my need for solitude. I had plenty of interaction with people in my school, work and play so when I had *free* time I liked to read. Mother would chide me, on a Sunday afternoon, when my friends were doing whatever they did, I was at home with a book. It seemed like a harmless pastime to me. Mother liked to socialize.

Mother went by herself to visit family and friends in Alberta, I believe in 1944, by train. She was to return at 3:00 a.m. on a certain morning and my father was going to pick her up at the Newton train station, seven miles away. I was sleeping soundly when suddenly I was awakened by my mother saying "The train came in early and I got a ride with someone else, but just as I came in the front door I saw Papa leaving to pick me up. Could you take the pickup and try to intercept him?" I jumped out of bed with only my shorts on, ran down the stairs and out the back door, jumped into the 1940 Ford pickup and headed for Newton. I gradually became aware that I might have a dilemma. I had nothing on but my shorts, driving to Newton to intercept my dad— was this a dream or what? What if I didn't catch up to him before he got to Newton? Fortunately in about three miles I caught up to him cruising leisurely and honked and waved him to the side of the road. It all ended well and I returned to dreamland for a little while.

In 1946 we moved to South Main and Dad bought into Uncle Titus's slaughtering business. Uncle Titus had lockers that he rented out to persons who needed frozen storage. It was just after the war and home freezers were still unknown. The business was right north of the Hesston State Bank. (The building was demolished when the bank expanded.) They primarily slaughtered beef for persons who wanted fresh meat and brought their own critter to be slaughtered. They would hang the carcasses in a large cooler for aging and then cut up the meat, usually for placing in the lockers. I would occasionally help with the butchering when I was attending college. Since many individuals did not take the liver or heart it was rather a standard fare at our house —an excellent source of protein and cholesterol! One time a customer complained about the quality of the meat that had been processed and my father paid him for it and put it in our locker since he could not taste or see anything wrong with it. One evening my parents invited Lyle and Erma Yost to our place for supper and served some of this meat. Erma fussed about the meat saying "My, it must be nice to have a butchering business and get the pick of the meat." If only she knew. My mother never told her.

I have not mentioned my siblings very much during these years. Glenn did not participate very much in the farm labor. He did however start an interesting business after we moved to the college farm. I mentioned earlier in my narrative about a hot cereal that we had in Alberta called *Sunny Boy*. Nothing comparable was available in the U.S. so he decided to produce our own brand which he called *Morning Cheer*. He purchased the ingredients of cracked wheat, ground barley, ground rye and flax seed, as I recall. We had a large wooden tub into which he would measure the ingredients and then tumble them until they were thoroughly mixed. This operation was in the basement of our house on the college farm. He put the concoction into clear plastic bags with a label on the inside of the bag and sealed it. He took a load of these sacks in the car and peddled them to the grocery stores in about a twenty-five mile radius of Hesston. There were a number of patrons who got "hooked" on the product and he made it for several years. When he left home the business was taken over by I. Mark Ross. I don't think there was any exchange of funds for the business.

Glenn was hoping to go to Goshen College and enrolled there for one summer after completing his study at Hesston but the hot humidity of Goshen did not suit him and he did not feel well all summer. He then decided to go to Bethel College and lived at home while he completed his studies there. In 1946 he planted peas in the garden on January twenty-four. They actually did quite well although not as well as those planted later. He enjoyed experimenting. That summer he married Lois Diller. He did a good deal of soul searching as to whether he should marry but the medical people felt that he could live a long and productive life with proper care. He and Lois built a house on South Main. Although they had a nice house they never owned a car during their short time together. They usually went with our family to church and took my parents' car for errands. He started teaching math and physics at the college that year.

Pearl did well in school and was put on an accelerated program that moved her up one grade so she again was two years ahead of me. Since it took me two years of correspondence to complete my senior year she actually moved three grades ahead of me. She sang in choir and did some dating before Lloyd Rodgers found her. She had considered a career in nursing but I think Lloyd sidetracked that. They were married in December of 1945 on a night that was very cold and the furnace had not been started soon enough at church so the building was cold. Grandpa Brenneman had a heavy fur coat and he kept it on for the service. Martha and I were part of a singing group for the service. I still remember the dress Martha wore. The following day they had a large dinner reception in the basement of Green Gables at Hesston College. She was marrying a nice Christian gentleman who had money so mother didn't need to worry about her daughter being provided for.

John liked to deliver the milk to the college dining room which was in the basement of Green Gables. He knew all the girls and all the girls knew him. Shortly after he started to high school he discovered Grace Bontrager, a classmate, from Yoder, Kansas. Since it was not acceptable to date at such a tender age I believe they saw each other covertly. After a time they were able to start dating openly. John did not like to sing with the family and we told him that he was not going to get into choir if he didn't learn to sing. He informed us that when the time came he would get into choir. The first time he tried out he got in and became an excellent musician with a wonderful high tenor voice. Being the youngest, and a bit out of control, mother spent some extra time worrying and praying for him. He enjoyed perfecting his hook shot in basketball. He usually did this move without a ball. He asked me once, "How was my form on that one?" I replied, being the practical type, "Did the ball go in the hoop?" He also enjoyed broadcasting make-believe basketball games and could be heard around the house doing his play by play.

James was a good worker and could be counted on to do what needed to be done. He also enjoyed music and fluctuated between singing baritone and second tenor. He got into the choir also the first time he tried out. He was a good student and had an active social life. Neither James nor John was very athletic so did not participate in team sports to any great extent. James enjoyed sermon preparation while he was still in high school. He also bought the first radio and phonograph in our house. He was of a frugal nature and had a way of squirreling away funds that eluded John. He seemed to enjoy the "cupcake" girls and had some disappointments because they weren't always attracted to him. His older siblings tried to give him some advice on these matters but he mostly ignored our advice. Later on he found Gladys Kauffman, a very nice looking young lady who became the love of his life.

In the late summer of 1945 Ralph Vogt, a local farmer whom I would sometimes work for, was doing custom combining in North Dakota and the individual that was driving his tractor had to return to school. He asked me if I could come up to Parshall, North Dakota to take his place. I considered it a good option so I boarded the bus at Hesston and in a combination of bus and train rides found my way to Minot, ND where

Ralph picked me up. It was a new adventure for a lad who had never before taken public transportation to find his way. In three days time I was on site ready to go to work. The gentleman who ran the combine was old enough to be my father but was nothing like my father. We attended church together and I would be asked if he was my father. He was an unabashed flirt. He would find a likely maiden lady and would make the clumsiest attempts to attract her attention. I was embarrassed for both of us! He later married and has long since gone to his reward but I was glad when we were combining that summer and not socializing. There was a lot of rain that late summer so to earn additional money, as well as fill the time, I hired out to a local farmer. I received some additional education without needing to pay tuition. I enjoyed eating in the local café and got to know some of the other harvesters stranded in the area. We eventually were able to complete the harvest and I returned to Hesston.

In the summer of 1946 I worked with Ephraim Risser, a member of our church, who was a carpenter. I use the term carpenter rather than builder because he was a very modest man and would consider the term "builder" a notch above where he considered himself. I learned a lot that summer. We built a barn for George Sommerfeld. Amy, his wife, always provided a feast for the noon meal. I think she might have wearied of us by the end of the summer but she didn't show it. For a number of years Ephraim did not take communion because he felt unworthy due to unresolved issues with one or more of the members. Rather than *hide* he openly shared his discomfort. His wonderful frankness and honesty resonated with me in a special way. His wife, Emma, never seemed to have a faith doubt in her life and I always felt she was partly to blame for his feelings of inadequacy. He was a most conscientious and careful worker who taught me a great deal. He later came to peace with his brother in the church and was able to participate in communion again.

When the barn was completed James and I painted the shingles on the roof. It was very steep so we put ropes across the peak of the roof to hold the two by six that we were standing on. We were busy painting when all of a sudden the rope on James's side came loose and he went sliding off the roof. I was hanging on but he slid off and I heard a crunch, a crash and a thump. The swinging barn door was open where he fell and he tore it from its hinges, which helped break his fall, and then he continued on down to the ground. He was not severely hurt and after re-securing the rope we continued on our way with only his sore stomach and a half gallon of spilt paint poorer for the event.

I was invited by Gene Weaver, Milf Weaver and Don Cooprider to take a trip to Hot Springs, AR in the fall of 1945. We all had farm deferments but Milf had been summoned to take his physical for induction into the draft. Gene's Dad had a new Oldsmobile that we used for the trip. We had a good time. It was a bit unusual at the time to see four grown boys out of uniform traveling together. These fellows were not close friends of mine so I was a bit surprised when they asked me to accompany them but I appreciated their invitation. I never socialized with them very often after this single foray except for Don Cooprider.

I left the high school years with some questions. Do I really want to become a doctor? Will Martha marry me if I don't? Where will the Lord lead me? What does He want me to do?

Musings on the Hesston Academy Years

The move from Mazeppa to Hesston was a cosmic shift in my small universe. My world, though very confined by many standards, exploded. I had all kinds of options that I only dreamt about when living in Alberta. Although still poor, we never felt the real pinch of poverty that we experienced in Alberta. We had a small and steady income that started to increase when we moved to the college farm.

During these years I met the wonderful girl that I later married, I had decided on a life work, I had opportunity for learning never before afforded to me. I was developing an appreciation for good music and some skill in making music such as the opportunity to lead singing in our local church. My circle of friends had increased immeasurably, particularly those who had like convictions and values. I grew spiritually and in understanding of my life's direction. I was still naïve but also idealistic and felt that I could make a difference in the world. I continued to develop good work habits that were valuable later on. Because school work was relatively easy I didn't develop very good study habits. I could get *decent* grades without a great deal of effort. I became informed about the larger church and had the privilege of meeting many of the church leaders of our own denomination. These were growing and knowing years.

The College Years (1946-50)

I entered Hesston College in the fall of 1946 after being out of school for two years. Martha was now a classmate of mine again and we dated regularly through our college years. What a wonderful prize! Since I was on a pre-med track I took a number of chemistry and biology courses. At the beginning of the year all of the freshmen had to take an entrance test for our proficiency in the English language to determine if we would need to take English grammar or if we would get to take English literature. Martha's sister Alice was in the English department and when asked, "How did I do on my exam?" she replied, "Very poorly, but you were in the upper half so you will take English literature." English grammar was never a favorite subject for me.

I was again in the college choir. J. P. Duerksen had returned from his leave due to the draft and we again had a capable choir director. I also sang in a men's quartet. I'm not totally certain as to how we got together but I believe Earl Greaser and I wanted to find a second tenor and a high tenor and looked around until we found Evan Oswald and Norman Teague. We practiced a couple times a week. One of the limitations of the

(Fred, Evan, Earl, Norman, Howard – 1947)

day was that we never practiced with a piano. This was one of the reasons we were not always as true to pitch as we should have been. Martha admitted (privately) that she didn't think we were especially good. We also had some trouble with blend because our voices were too different and we tended to pronounce our words differently. Earl and I were from the same genetic barrel so usually agreed on interpretation and pronunciation. In spite of this we became the primary men's quartet for the college and traveled extensively during our two years together. We were kindred spirits and had similar values so we enjoyed each other spiritually and socially as well as musically.

Our quartet made various short weekend trips to neighboring states during my freshman year. We decided to follow the harvest the summer of 1947 and sing as we had opportunity. Milo Kauffman, the president of the college, heard about our plans and asked us if we would travel on behalf of the college and they would pay us $500 each for the assignment. We unanimously agreed. The Young Peoples Christian Association at the college, had just purchased a 1946 Ford station wagon with wood paneling on the sides. It was a classy rig. They agreed, somewhat reluctantly, at the urging of the college administration, to let us drive this vehicle for the summer. The college selected Fred Erb, a Bible student who was a year ahead of us and a little older, to be the sponsor and deliver the messages on behalf of the college. Fred Erb was a couple years older than us but it would be a stretch to say he was more mature!

On the first half of the summer we went to the west coast then up into Alberta and Saskatchewan then down through Montana, the Dakotas, Minnesota, Iowa and back home for a change of clothes. We were home

(me at Grand Canyon on tour)

for only a couple days and then proceeded to the east coast and up into Ontario before returning to Hesston. We traveled just over 15,000 miles. It was a lot of windshield time and a lot of togetherness. We gave programs virtually every week night and usually three on Sunday. We also sang on the radio in Illinois on a Christian radio show.

We had a number of memorable moments. We were coming through Idaho; Fred was driving, and drove off the side of the road into a rocky ditch, severely scratching the passenger door panels. It was one of the rare times we didn't have a program in the evening. The next evening we were going to be in Kalispell, MT where Norman Kauffman, who was the chairman of the YPCA at the college, lived. He had been unfavorable to us taking the car for the summer. Fred was able to get the car into a body shop and we put in some night driving to make it to Kalispell with the car looking quite pristine.

Fred Erb was from Ontario, Canada and was in Hesston on a student visa. The visa had expired and he was going to get it renewed when we got back to Ontario. The problem was that we had come back into Canada in Alberta and were leaving through Saskatchewan with an expired visa. When we got to the U.S. customs the customs official leaned in the window and after asking what we were doing asked, "Are any of you Canadians?" Fred immediately piped up "Howard, you were born in Canada, weren't you?" to which I readily assented. I had my papers with me showing my U.S. citizenship and I went into my suitcase and retrieved it. No more was said and we sailed off into the U.S. Evan Oswald was particularly incensed at what he considered to be a blatant lie. Fred defended himself, as best he could, by saying he never said an untruth, just left a truth unsaid. Evan would not talk to Fred for a couple days after the escapade. Evan was an ardent sportsman and fisherman so when we got to Minnesota and were entertained at my Uncle Elmer's place, my cousin Frank took Evan out on the fishing boat. Evan didn't have either a fishing pole or a license to fish but he was in the boat. They ran into a school of bluegill and Frank was pulling them in as fast as he could throw the line into the water. Evan was tempted above what he was able to bear and took the fishing tackle and pulled a number of fish into the boat. Needless to say, Evan lost his credibility with Fred for fishing without a license.

When we were at Fisher, IL we gave a program to a full house. There were four chairs on the platform and there were five of us so they brought a folding chair for me. We gave the first section of our program but when

I went back to my chair it collapsed and I landed on the floor. I was not injured and the audience seemed to enjoy it.

When we got back to Canada, this time in Ontario, we had a day of leisure as Fred was going to Toronto to get his visa extended. His father worked as a greenskeeper at a very nice golf course in Kitchener and he arranged for us to play golf for the day. None of us had ever held a golf club in our hands. Evan had opined during the trip since he was the best athlete of our group (probably true) given a completely new game none of us had ever played, he would win. This was the true test. Final score was Earl, first, Howard, second, Evan, third, and Norman, fourth. Either the theory was wrong or Evan wasn't the best natural athlete. We ended with a hung jury!

Fred had six different sermons that he preached and each of the quartet members thought they could have delivered any one of them by the time the summer was over in the event he became ill. We never got the chance. We had a secret sign for when he went on too long, it was folding our arms and laying two fingers across our sleeve. We got to use it on a number of occasions.

We sang to full houses almost every place we went. The war was ended, gas rationing was over and concerts were rare so they were ready to listen. All the money raised above our expenses was to be used to purchase furnishings for the new Hess Hall. We brought in substantially more than our expenses including paying a mileage fee to the YPCA!

At Christmas of 1947 we took a trip going through the Deep South from Texas to Florida. Several events stand out. We had a mature adult, Ivan Lind plus his wife Ethel, accompanying us. All six of us were crammed into Ivan's 1941 Ford sedan. When we got to Crowley, LA we stopped to give a program. The man in charge of the small congregation said Milo Kauffman had written telling him a quartet was coming but since he didn't know how many to expect he didn't arrange for a program! That night we stayed at a motel, an unusual event since we always stayed in homes. We had a free evening so we decided to go Christmas caroling. We were in a very nice part of Crowley and about the third house we sang at they were having a party. The host came out onto the lawn and invited us in for dinner and to join the party. They were a group of Southern Baptist young couples who were having a Christmas party. The group had already eaten but two black maids served us a delicious turkey dinner plus pecan pie and then asked us to give them a program. It was a memorable event of southern hospitality.

When we got to Sarasota, FL we gave a program at the Bayshore Mennonite Church. It was a standing-room-only crowd. Our crowds had been small for the whole trip, since the churches were small so Ivan decided to give them the whole load. He did an exposition from one of the Psalms translating from the original Hebrew and by the time he was done we had our fingers out on our sleeves. Rather than quit he dissected another Psalm. When the service was over he was appalled at the small offering. These were rich snow birds from the North and he thought they would be very generous. Ethel told him frankly, "You talked too long." Since she said it we didn't need to. I also came to a tentative conclusion the "snow birds" might not be particularly generous when they are on their winter roost.

Ivan had slept a lot that day in anticipation of driving straight home to Hesston. He didn't last until midnight and when he stopped for gas he asked Norman to drive. Norman had grown up in the Kansas City Children's Home and had really never learned to drive very well at this time. I heard him ask Norman so I immediately volunteered for the front center location where I could supervise. It was a harrowing experience. Evan had been sleeping in the back seat but when he saw who was driving he was on full alert. Through the winding roads Norman would start around a vehicle and then just hang in the passing lane. I was not bashful about giving him instructions about what was safe and what wasn't! The Lord's angels were working overtime. When we stopped for gas Ivan said, "Norm, are you ready to go again?" He was, and we had another go at it. Ivan was comfortably asleep in the back seat. With Norman driving none of the quartet members got sleepy. I think Norman drove more miles that night than he had in his whole life before. During our summer trip Fred, Earl and I did the driving. I believe Fred didn't ask Evan because he didn't want to single Norman out as the only one not asked to drive. We will never know.

My parents had moved into the house they built in 1945 and my father worked at the Hesston Locker during my years in college. Tuition was the paltry sum of about $200 per year so paying for a year of college was not a strain.

Without farm chores to do I quite often worked on Saturdays with the Vogt farms, usually either Willard or Ralph. I also worked at the locker during the week when I wasn't busy in school.

(James, Mother, Glenn, Pearl, Howard, Dad, John—1946. Glenn needed to wear clerical collar to teach at Hesston)

I continued my unexamined pursuit toward a medical vocation taking all of the chemistry and biology courses available at Hesston. I was a good student though not a great one and I got mostly A's with a smattering of B's. For the record, C was much closer to the average than it is today. I don't believe that it is because kids are brighter today. Grades have crept up as students and parents have put the pressure on teachers to be more lenient.

When I returned from my trip in the summer of 1947 Martha and I became convinced that we were meant for each other and that the Lord was leading in the direction of marriage so we became engaged but did not immediately announce it. We started making plans to marry the following summer in spite, or maybe because, of the long school road ahead. When we made our engagement announcement I was thrown into the pool on the back side of the campus known as the Bird Sanctuary. It was wonderful! I had asked Martha's father for her hand and he had a rather frank talk with me. I believe he thought that it would take more than LOVE to finance our marriage. Martha and I hadn't given the money part very much thought. We knew we wanted to be married and live together and have children. Why have concerns about money? I guess we convinced him we could live on love because he gave his blessing. My parents liked Martha, trusted me, and didn't seem overly concerned about our financial future.

When our quartet traveled during the summer I was the one that put on the most weight. I was used to eating a lot but I was also used to working a lot so this was the first experience of this imbalance. My fellow quartet members gave me the endearing nickname of "Lard." After we announced our engagement a number of students who had gone from Hesston to Goshen sent us a congratulatory telegram. Fred Erb's message was "Lard's melted." I lost the fifteen pounds I had gained after I got back to home cooking and home working.

During the summer of 1948 I purchased our first car, a 1937 Chevrolet. It had been ridden hard and put to bed wet too many times but it served us for a few years. This was one of several disappointments for my father-in-law. He was a Ford man and I know he would have liked to help me find a car. I was probably too insecure to let him. Martha was graduating with a major in elementary education and was able to secure a teaching position at Zimmerdale grade school with a sixty-hour certificate. It appeared that at least our first year would be taken care of. After graduating I worked in carpentry again with Ephraim Risser. Martha stayed at home getting ready for our wedding, planning, sewing and gardening. On Sunday morning August 15, 1948 we made the trip down the aisle. The whole church was invited and

(Martha and Howard –
August 15, 1948)

we convinced our parents to let us reverse the normal order of service so that Sunday school could be first and our wedding would replace the normal preaching service. There was a lot of congregational singing with the main special group being a ladies quartet Martha had been a part of. Both of Martha's brothers sang solos accompanied by the quartet. Martha's sister Esther and my brother James stood with us and then when we knelt after the ceremony we sang *Gracious Father,* a short song of benediction. After the ceremony our families ate together at Martha's parents' place. At three in the afternoon we had a reception in the church basement.

After the reception we drove to Wichita to the Lassen Hotel, the premier hotel at that time and got an air conditioned room for $4.75. Martha kept the receipt—a source of kidding from Martha is that I signed the register as Howard Hershberger and wife!! The next morning we were out fairly early (old habits die hard,) and went to a small café close to the hotel for breakfast. The sausage was partially spoiled so the breakfast left a great deal to be desired. A family tradition, acknowledged only, is that we have spoiled sausage for breakfast the morning after our wedding anniversaries. We spent some time in Riverside Park and then got some groceries and headed back to Hesston. Martha kept the receipt from our first grocery shopping expedition—forty-nine items for a grand total of $9.80!

Our first apartment was in the upstairs of my parents' home on South Main. There was a small kitchen, bathroom, bedroom and dining-living room. A second bedroom was occupied by James and John who also shared the bath with us. There was an open stairway to the lower floor so privacy was at a premium. We did not have a refrigerator so Mother gave us one shelf of her refrigerator. This was the home we went to after our honeymoon of one night and day. It is amazing what one can put up with for LOVE. There was a built-in desk in our bedroom so the bedroom door could be locked by pulling the drawer part way open. This was my bedroom before we were married so I didn't "leave father and mother and cleave unto my wife." I did the latter but didn't leave home!

Shortly after we set up housekeeping we were both immersed in school. Milf and Rosie Roupp were married in Greensburg, KS the week before we were and also lived in Hesston. They had a better car than we did and both of us were pre-med juniors at Bethel College. Rosie was teaching at a grade school east of Newton so they would pick us up, drop Martha off at Zimmerdale, drop Milf and me

(Esther, Martha, Howard, James – Wedding party)

off at Bethel and Rosie would continue on to her school. In the evening this scenario would be repeated in reverse order. This was probably the first time since grade school I was "stuck" in school for the whole day. I spent a lot of time in the library and read LOTS of books. I had heard on the Del Rio, TX radio station about a contest being sponsored by *The Southern Farmer* magazine. How many four letter words could you make out of ***The Southern Farmer Prints the Truth?*** The first prize was $10,000 and the second was a new Buick. They said what dictionary was going to be used, which was the unabridged dictionary they had in the library so I went through the whole dictionary and found every four letter word using those letters. This was not as difficult as one might think and in a week or so in my spare time I completed the assignment and sent it in. I did not receive the prize. How could that be? It was an open book test— I wrote and asked for a list of the winners. Apparently they thought I had the answer sheet!! So much for the Southern Farmer Printing the Truth!

I enjoyed my class work. A particular favorite of mine was L. C. Kreider, who taught Chemistry. I found out he was going to Akron, OH the following year so I took all of my chemistry courses my junior year. I developed some good friends from the General Conference Mennonite Church during the two years I attended Bethel.

Shortly after the school year began it turned cold and Martha had to learn to start a coal burning furnace with kindling wood. It was a new learning for her but she soon became good at it. Since she was the first one left off she got there early enough to get the fire going and getting it warm before the students arrived. Of more significance is that she became pregnant shortly after school began so life became a bit more difficult. She had a normal pregnancy and although the school board was a bit concerned about an obviously pregnant woman teaching she was able to complete the school year which ended in the latter part of April. Gwendolyn June was born on June 3, 1949.

Brother Glenn had a very difficult winter and had to take time off from his teaching because of health problems. He had begun teaching again but was still in some respiratory distress. On Saturday, April 23, I went over to his house, only two doors away, and he was puttering around outside. He told me after some visiting, "I'm not going to be able to live any more; I'm so sorry for Lois." I made an attempt to tell him he felt that way because he was depressed about his current ill health. He said that it was different this time. On Monday, April 25, I came home from school earlier than normal and was told that Glenn had dropped over in his physics classroom and was gone. The county school superintendent,

Florence Michaels, was visiting in his class that day. She said later she always enjoyed attending his classes because he made math and physics interesting for the students. He had a good sense of humor and a good imagination. It was a very large funeral held in the college chapel. It seemed very unreal that he was no longer with us.

Their daughter Glenna Joy was born on May 19, 1949. Lois continued to come to the Pennsylvania church in the country, and later Whitestone in town, the rest of her life, even though her family all attended the College Mennonite Church. Lois became employed as a secretary for the new Hesston Manufacturing Company and worked there continuously except for one year when she served as secretary to Roy Roth, president of Hesston College. She retired some time in the 1990s. Glenna Joy stayed with my mother when Lois worked and Lois always had lunch with my parents and Glenna at noon. Later, when Glenna started to school, mother's home was where Glenna went after classes. I don't think Lois ever considered another marriage.

Gwendolyn was a most unusually smiley baby. She carried her emotions on her sleeve and would give the big smile very easily and also cry easily when things didn't go her way. Martha, of course, stayed

home to take care of her. It was never a consideration, in those days, for a mother to work outside the home when they had a small child. Martha adjusted easily to motherhood. It was much more fun than teaching all eight grades in a country grade school. In spite of a brochure touting the college education curriculum which showed a picture of Martha with the caption, *I would rather be a teacher than anything else in the world,* Martha enjoyed teaching her own children but not in the classroom. Death again came knocking. That fall, just after Gwen's six-month birthday, she became seriously ill. We had taken

(Emoting Gwendolyn – six months) her to the doctor and he felt it was a severe case of the flu. It indeed was serious. On the night of December 15 we were up all night with her and finally in the early morning hours took her to Bethel Hospital in Newton. The doctor saw her immediately but was unable to save her. She died early the morning of the 16th. One does not go through those experiences without doing some soul searching and asking questions. Should we have insisted that she be hospitalized when we took her to the doctor? Were we negligent in other ways? You never completely recover from the death of a child. We still remember her bright smile and sunny disposition. We had her little casket in the south window of our living room. Many friends came by and many kind words were given and received. One individual stated, "I know just how you feel, my elderly father-in-law died last week." NEVER say you know *exactly* how someone else feels; you don't, even if you have gone through a similar experience!

The senior year at Bethel was somewhat different. Milf Roupp decided on a different course so he was no longer enrolled at Bethel. I now drove to school so I was free to return to Hesston when I didn't have classes. This gave me more opportunity to work since Martha was no longer supporting us. I worked primarily at the locker in Hesston but also occasionally at Hesston Manufacturing Company. An interesting sidelight of my time working in the shop at Hesston Corporation was singing at break time. Some of the Holdeman men brought men's choir books to work and we would sing together. It was fun and we had a small audience.

I took mostly biology courses my senior year plus a few other courses that were required. One of these was Spanish because you needed a foreign language at that time to get into medical school. Our teacher was Mrs. Warkentine. She had been a translator at the Nuremburg trials and was a good linguist but a very naïve teacher. She was the only college teacher I had who let the students be in charge. Some of the fellows regularly skipped class and she thought it was necessary to give excuses for them. I could have told her why they weren't there but she didn't ask. In the fall of 1949 I took my entrance exams for medical school at Wichita University. I also had an interview at Kansas University. In the late winter of 1950 I was informed that I had been accepted. I gave a sigh of relief. Nationally the class of 1950 was a huge class because it included all of the GI's who started to college after the war. KU medical school had 365 applicants for 100 positions. A good friend of Martha's had better grades than I did and hadn't made the cut. (She was admitted the following year and became a medical doctor.)

In the spring quarter I had the liberty of taking any course that I wanted because I had met all my graduation requirements. It may be telling that I chose an advanced course on the history of England rather than another course offered for my major. If I would have looked more closely at my real interests I would have had doubts about my career direction.

A project that I undertook during my senior year was the disassembly and the reconstruction of a large rooster for a biology class. I purchased a very mature rooster and de-feathered and gutted it. I then put it in the pressure cooker to thoroughly cook it. The meat was OK, if not prime, and after taking most of the meat off the bones I continued to cook it until I was able to get all of the meat off. After completing this process I bleached the bones and then reassembled the carcass using various gauges of wire to hold the bones together where there had been muscle and sinew. After it was completely assembled I mounted it on a stand for display. It turned out very well. It stood in a display case in the Biology Lab at Bethel College for a couple decades. Since this was all done in our small kitchen, and Martha was pregnant it wasn't the most pleasant project from her point of view.

As mentioned earlier, we had access to free beef liver. One time Martha was fixing a nice dinner of liver and onions, mashed potatoes and gravy and she mentioned that she wished she had some *Kitchen Bouquet* to make the gravy a little darker. How a meal was presented was always very important to her. I thought I had the answer so I put in a dash of red food coloring. It was a BIG mistake. Liver, for a pregnant Martha, was very close to the boundary but a livid pink liver was WAY outside the boundary. I apologized for quite a while. I did eat the mashed potatoes with bright pink gravy but I needed to keep my eyes focused elsewhere.

Oral comps that spring were also memorable. There was considerable rivalry between the natural and social science departments and when a natural science major was being interviewed the social science examiner would try to show him or her up. This of course was reciprocated attempting to show that the graduating candidate didn't have a complete world view. I didn't really care if I impressed them favorably or not because I had already been admitted to medical school. My science professor gave me a lot of softball questions I could expound on but the social science teacher talked completely over my head. I don't remember the particulars but he asked me about what a certain person, who I had never heard of, thought about a certain subject. I replied "I never heard of the individual so naturally I have no opinions on what he thought." I believe the interview ended on that note and I was cleared for graduation.

Kansas University accepted a class of one-hundred but only had room for seventy-five at any given time on the Lawrence campus. I opted to start immediately after graduation because we were expecting another child in September of 1950 and I wanted the fall term off. I went off to KU and Martha stayed with her parents in Hesston. I roomed with Clayton Diener, who was seven years older than I. His wife, Inez, also was not in Lawrence so we roomed together at the *Henry House*. It was a co-op and we did our own cooking, cleaning, etc. Willard Kaufman, a second-year medical student also lived there. He later practiced medicine in Moundridge for a number of years. I acquired some local fame for my cake baking. Everyone used cake mix when they baked but not Howard; he baked from scratch. Pineapple upside down cake was a favorite. There were about twenty-four men in the house and duties were assigned by the head honcho.

The study was tremendously intense as all these aspiring doctors were vying for top grades. I took gross anatomy and remember the name of the gentleman we dissected. Earl Grey had been a tall and thin black man. I remember the name of the cadaver but don't remember the name of my lab partner. What can you make of that?

I also found out there is an incredible amount of memory work in medicine. Learning all of the anatomical names was a challenge. I marveled at Clayton Diener, my roommate, who could spell these long anatomical names but couldn't spell the simplest words in the English language so I would help him with the spelling in his letters to Inez and he would help me with the anatomical names. Evan Oswald was checking into taking some graduate school work at KU and came to visit us. We were too busy studying to do much visiting. I had no idea when he left or what was said—my mind was elsewhere. I also took a less demanding course that summer in psychology that was taught by some doctors from the Menninger Clinic in Topeka. Carl Menninger lectured a couple times and I found him very fascinating. He kept his audience alert.

Martha visited me once and I went back to Hesston once during the summer. We wrote letters but did not phone each other. We were living in two completely different worlds. I had never been so preoccupied in my entire life. Martha had trouble reaching me, I think. We had a joint checking account and due to lack of communication, and money, we got an overdraft. Martha had no access to money and Howard had no access to money. I remember the almost desperate feeling I had. I contacted Dad and he took care of it for us.

I had the fall off. During the prior year I had helped with the building of the Village Motel which my parents were erecting where the current Casey's convenience store is located. I had laid tile for that job and also some other places so it seemed like a good opportunity to earn some money while waiting to go back to school. One of the jobs was for the office of Hesston Manufacturing and I enjoyed the interaction I experienced there with the employees.

On September 24 John Howard was born. As became the custom for Martha, she named him as soon as he parted the womb and she was told the sex. I had picked the name for our first born, Gwendolyn, but Martha bestowed the name immediately after birth. John was a healthy bouncing boy and Martha had her arms full once more.

Martha had moved to her parents' place while I was in medical school but when I returned for the summer we decided to buy a trailer house that could be moved to Lawrence, and then later to Kansas City. We moved the twenty-eight foot trailer to a spot behind the Village Motel where they had a utility hook-up. To have our own four walls for the first time was a momentous occasion. Even though the shower showered all over the stainless steel bathroom it was HOME!

I immediately started seriously looking for funds to continue in school. Neither the banks nor the government were in the business of student loans so I needed to look elsewhere. Uncle Fred was a prime target but he seemed pretty cool to the idea without directly turning me down. I then contacted a couple large-scale farmers. I think my dad could have found the person or persons to fund my education but I didn't ask him and he didn't volunteer. I guess he thought if I was mature enough to get married and have a family that I should be mature enough to find my own money.

The upshot was that two days before I was to return to Lawrence I withdrew from school. I still have the letter from KU releasing me but because I had completed only one summer term I would need to reapply if I wanted to continue later. I never planned on continuing. When Uncle Fred found out I had withdrawn he told me he could have furnished the money if he had known I was that desperate. I have no recollection of either my parents or Martha's parents commenting on my dropping out. It was my decision to go so it was my decision not to go. I felt, probably unjustifiably, father Earl didn't hold me in very high regard so was not surprised that I bailed out.

What to do?? James, after teaching one year at the Zimmerdale School where Martha taught, had decided he was not a teacher. He went to work as an accountant at the fledgling Hesston Manufacturing Co. He was subject to the draft during the Korean War so was going into I-W service in Kansas City. Lyle Yost, the president of the company, found out I was no longer going to medical school so contacted me and asked if I would do the accounting, at least while James was gone. Although I had a number of math courses and enjoyed them I told him that I had never taken any accounting, not even high school bookkeeping. "Accounting is very easy," he said. "It is basically addition and subtraction, some multiplication and division and they have certain conventions you need to follow, but it's really quite simple." He convinced me I was qualified and I took up the offer. I was planning on doing it until James returned and then I would find something else. I didn't realize I had a tiger by the tail. There were thirty-three employees when I started; there were 3500, worldwide, when I resigned twenty-five years later.

I left the college years with some questions. Why did Glenn have to die in the midst of a productive life? Why was Gwendolyn taken from us when only starting life? What was I going to do to earn a living? Am I really a failure since I feel like one?

Musings about my college years

These were four momentous years—marriage, death, birth and death and another birth. I married Martha, the girl of my dreams; I lost Glenn, a best friend, brother, mentor and confidant who died at the young age of twenty-nine. We were blest with a loving, happy baby girl, Gwendolyn, and suddenly she was gone at just over six months of age. We felt rewarded with the arrival of a bouncing baby boy.

I had a major change in occupational direction as one door closed and I was unsure about what other door was opening. Financially we learned to get along with very little. These lessons learned stayed with us and shaped us for the rest of our lives.

We acquired lifelong friends during these days—friends that both of us have enjoyed all of the years since. We were thrust into making adult decisions without direct supervision from our parents. I started learning what it meant to say "we" instead of "I." Sharing a life together with my very best friend was especially important during some turbulent life events.

The Hesston Corporation Years
(1951-76)

I started working for the company in January, 1951. I immediately enrolled in a program offered by the National Accounting Society for practicing accountants who needed additional training. I discovered immediately that I really resonated with the disciplines of accounting. Although I worked quite long hours I still enjoyed doing the course work after hours. Accounting just seemed to fit the shape of my head whereas biology and chemistry never seemed like a good fit. The Lord had been leading.

A policy, quickly abandoned for later employees, was for office employees to start in the shop for at least a month before working in the office. For the first month of my employment I worked in various positions in the plant. I was awed by how slowly time went by. I would decide that I would not look up at the clock but finally thinking that an hour must have passed I would look up and see that ten minutes had gone by. Experiencing what employees did working in the plant made me a much more compassionate manager later on. Years later, when we were negotiating with the union, the union president said, "Howard, you don't have any idea what it's like to work at a machine all day for five dollars per hour." I replied, "You're right, but I do know what it was like to work at a machine all day for seventy-five cents an hour."

I was the only employee in the accounting department when I started and sales were under one million dollars. Most of the billing and all of the posting to the ledgers was done by hand so clerical efficiency was vital. Producing the monthly financial reports was a major challenge so I needed to burn some midnight oil to get them all done. Martha was very understanding. Her father worked exceedingly long hours as a mechanic so it was no stretch for her to believe I needed to do the same.

In the fall of my first year of employment I got a very severe case of mumps that infected more than my throat glands and I was off work for about ten days. James was able to get free for a few days from his assignment in Kansas City for part of that time to take care of the most critical needs. I was still the only employee in accounting and the company was extremely busy that fall because a new product had been introduced. The receipts for money received were all thrown into the middle drawer of my desk but none of the billing had been done when I returned. It almost caused a relapse. I worked like a dog to get caught up. We added a clerk at that time and then later Don Cooprider was hired as an additional accountant. When James came back from I-W he set up the cost accounting system and worked in that area for a couple years.

Daniel Glenn was born in the fall, just thirteen months younger than John so Martha had some extra work to keep her occupied. He was dark skinned with lots of black hair which grew low on his forehead. After I had decided not to continue in medical school we moved into my sister-in-law's upstairs apartment. It was there that John said his first sentence, "I want to go down."

We purchased a new car that fall, a 1951 Chevrolet. The only accessory it had was a spare tire, no radio or other goodies. I paid full retail in cash—the sum of $1900. Again, I disappointed my father-in-law by not buying a Ford. Since we had only one car Martha was left at home without transportation so I usually picked up the groceries after work. Martha had given me a list of items she wanted. Her list included yellow jello, red jello and green jello. Mary Swartzendruber ran a restaurant across the street from the grocery store and I asked her where the jello was. I showed her the list and commented "Martha asks for jello by the color, not the flavor; she is really a better artist than a cook." It was a cheap shot. Martha was an excellent cook but she also always had an eye for color.

In December of 1951 we tried out our new car by driving to Goshen for the marriage of James to Gladys Kauffman. John was a lap baby because Martha had to hold him, sitting in the middle of the front seat, at least on the way back. Daniel, only two months old, stayed in Hesston with Grandpa and Grandma Buckwalter.

The following spring I was asked to sing the bass solo for the annual presentation of *The Holy City*. The college was able to find, in their archives, a picture of the whole choir. The tenor soloist and I stood out because we were the only men with jackets. It was the last time the college performed it without piano accompaniment. I think that J. P. Duerksen was desperate to find a bass soloist. It was still an honor to be asked.

There were some lean years for the young manufacturing company. The first product was a combine unloading auger to unload grain without needing to stop. Lyle had been a custom combine operator and saw the need. He took his idea to the local blacksmith, Aden Holdeman, and they developed it and started producing it. The clutch design was faulty and when the grain was damp the clutch would slip and the farmer would have a bin full of

(Our first house on South Main)

grain with no way to unload it. They soon were able to design a fix but if they replaced all of them at company expense the company would be bankrupt. There were voices who said, "Take your money and run" but Lyle said, "We will contact the owners and ask them to pay part of the cost of the fix, forty-nine dollars, so everyone can get their units fixed." Almost all of the owners agreed and paid the forty-nine dollars. The individuals who wouldn't pay were let off the hook without heavy pressure from the company. This strategy saved the company, no doubt. 1954 was the first year sales exceeded a million dollars. Because our sales were seasonal we were sometimes short on cash and both Lyle Yost and Harold Dyck, the sales manager, had their checks held several times so we would have enough money to meet the payroll. It was also during this period when I turned down a raise because I didn't think the company could afford it. A couple years later I asked for an increase so I decided I was even. I refused one and I asked for one. I don't believe I ever asked for an increase the rest of my working life.

We started building a house on South Main (where else would you build a house?) in the fall of 1952. We secured a loan of $5000 from Lloyd Nebergall, through my father. Lloyd had also helped finance the Village Motel and seemed to like my dad. Our plan was to complete the structure but only finish the basement. Ivan Diller was the builder. Before we shingled the roof in the latter part of October we had a giant snow storm. We did a lot of shoveling to get the snow out of the house before it melted and caused water damage. We were living in the basement of the house when our next child was born.

In April of 1953 Philip Earl was born. He looked like an Old Testament prophet when he was born, rather wrinkled and frowning. He was blond headed and just looked "prophetic." It might have been because he grew face hair later—it was a harbinger of things to come. A little over a year later he embarrassed me. In June of 1954 my cousin Thelma Brenneman married Larry Lais and we attended the wedding. Larry handed out cigars after the wedding and when he offered one to me I told him I could take it out of circulation if he wanted me to. I stuck it into the inside pocket of my suit coat. I didn't wear a suit coat in the summer and that fall I put it back on. We were sitting in church, well up toward the front and Philip was standing on my lap. He reached into my pocket and pulled out this nice big round item and started waving it for all the people behind us to see. Being an otherwise stand-up guy I was able to tell the story behind the cigar and stay in the fold!

We were ramping up for increased activity at Hesston Manufacturing. Although I was taking increased responsibility it was deemed by management that I was not ready to be the chief financial officer. In my heart I knew I wasn't ready but in my head I wanted to be. They hired Ray Schlichting for the position. He had gained considerable experience with MCC and with Miller-Hess Shoes as well as being wiser and more mature than I. I knew that it would be a stretch for me to grow fast enough to keep up with the company growth but it still was disappointing for the company to go outside to fill the position. I reported to Ray most of my working life at Hesston. He was an ideal supervisor and I learned a great deal, not only about accounting but also management, from him. He was an extremely important person in the growth and development of the company. Ray was Treasurer, Vice-President and CFO; I was the Controller with responsibility for all of the accounting functions, office management and later the computer operations. For a rapidly-growing company, I had my cup full. It was during the first year of Ray's tenure that I was having physical symptoms that were probably stress related. I was uptight, had difficultly relaxing, stomach aches and heart palpitations. Ray and I drove to Texas to see several companies that owed us money. It was also a time to plan. We spent an evening in Fort Worth and noticed *Charlie's Aunt* was playing at TCU. We went to the play and I laughed so hard that my insides got completely shaken loose and from then on I didn't have the symptoms. "Laughter doeth good like a medicine."

In May 1953 Brother John married Grace Bontrager at Yoder, Kansas. Our parents had the satisfaction of now having all of their children married to suitable Christian mates. Mother had enough concerns going forward for all of her children but we were aware that our parents were praying for us and our children as we journeyed forward on the path of life. Perhaps we were more appreciative of their concern after they were no longer with us.

We purchased a new dark green Ford Fairlane in the fall of 1954. It pleased Martha's dad immensely but caused me some additional discomfort. Whenever we would leave for a trip Dad B would pick up the car in the evening and return it, usually before midnight, fully tuned and ready to roll. My problem—I didn't quite know how to respond. Cars were made to run with just the prescribed maintenance and did not need any fine tuning, from my perspective. I wondered if he thought we were negligent in doing standard maintenance. Should I offer to pay him? It was all part of learning to relate to my father-in-law in an appropriate way. I never wondered if my sons-in-law had some of the same questions with my "interfering." This was a *hot* car and was the first automatic transmission car we had.

(Philip-one, Daniel-2, John-three)

We had now completed the upper floor of our home on South Main. Later, when my parents sold their motel by the highway, they built their home just south of us with one empty lot in between. Shortly, James and Gladys built a new brick home between us. With three of us together and Sister Lois across the street we presented a solid coalition. Others might have been a bit intimidated to enter our compound. It was too close for Martha because she felt every move and activity was being observed, particularly by my mother. James and I drilled a well for irrigation between our properties. For a little *"schputt"* instead of witching for water, I smelled along the ground until it smelled the wettest and there we drilled the well. We had a good supply of water, although extremely high in mineral content.

One of my extra jobs I took on was the treasurer position of the Rocky Mountain Mennonite Camp. Harold Dyck was the president of the board and we traveled together numerous times to the camp site. We would normally leave a little early from work and drive by car to Limon, CO for the night and then continue on to the camp the next morning. We would spend most of the day there and then return that evening. A learning from those times was on the subject of giving. Harold said he and Elva Mae had decided, because they had a good income (he was vice-president and sales manager at Hesston Manufacturing Company), they should give twenty percent of their gross income to charity. After talking to Martha about it, we decided we could do the same. It began a joyful experience for us. When I left Hesston Manufacturing Company and went to Hesston College with a third of the salary we did have to cut back to ten percent but when we went back into industry we again increased our giving. For the past number of years we have given over fifty percent of our income but our income has been greatly reduced in retirement. A case can be made for investing when you are younger so you can give more when you are older but I believe most of the time it doesn't happen that way.

Another extra job I took on during these years was serving on the Kiowa County Hospital Board at Greensburg, KS. This hospital was owned by the county but the Mennonite Church was hired to manage it. Again, I acquired some good friends through this association. We usually had our board meetings on Saturday so I was taking time away from Martha rather than from work.

The idea of leaving the business world and working for one of the church institutions was always a consideration. When the Mennonite Publishing Company at Scottdale, PA was looking for a CFO I was approached and sent in my resume. We had some additional conversation but it never went as far as an interview. Another foray was with Uncle Fred. He was thinking of building a medical clinic at Gasville, AR and he wanted me to be the business manager for the enterprise. Other than taking a trip to the site nothing more came of this. He never built the clinic. In looking back it is very apparent the life of service modeled for us children always kept me and my siblings with one foot in the business and one poised to do something more service oriented. Martha's family was also scattered all over the globe in various missionary or service occupations so it was a natural bent. James and Gladys made the move out of the business world some time in the 1950's and John and Grace also served at a hospital in Glenwood Springs. Lloyd and Pearl were tied to the farm and its challenges.

We continued to be very active in our local congregation. I served as chairman of our church for a couple terms, also served as treasurer for a period of time, sang in the choir that Martha started, with the encouragement of her dad, and was on the building committee when we moved our congregation to a new location in Hesston in 1964. Church attendance was always a top priority. Probably our children felt the church took precedence over them.

The first airplane ride in my life was on a Lockheed Constellation from Amarillo, TX to Wichita. I am unsure of the year but it was the beginning of many flights while I was employed at Hesston. Flying never was particularly exciting to me—getting to my destination was the important thing. Driving by car was more enjoyable—the trip was pleasurable, not just the destination. Driving was always relaxing for me and our family put in many hours on the road. Most of their memories of those times are good with a few other kinds of experiences mixed in.

In the late 1950s and early 1960s the company grew very rapidly. We were very busy in accounting trying to keep the wheels on the wagon. Our first calculators were Friden units that weighed about fifty pounds and covered a fourth of your desk. These units cost $1000 per copy and were extremely noisy. They did not have tapes so were used almost exclusively for multiplication and division. Before the advent of the electronic calculator it was the state of the art. We finally invested in a National Cash Register posting machine for posting to the ledgers to take some of the load off manually entering data by pen. This was a clumsy piece of equipment but was a stopgap measure.

We started looking seriously at computers in the early 1960s. The IBM Ramac 305 was introduced in 1956 and we saw one of their units at the Coleman Company in the late 1950s. Punch card technology was introduced in the 1930s and paired with computers in the 1940s but we felt that the random access technology of the Ramac was the wave of the future. Rather than spending effort on a punch card system we immediately opted for the IBM random access system. The unit we saw at Coleman was as large as a small railroad locomotive and required special cooling and climate control. We were not interested in that but in the early 60s they came out with units the size of a large washer or dryer with removable discs. Our first unit was installed in the early 60s. Good friend John Zielke headed up the effort. The first unit had only 4000 positions of core storage so you needed very frugal programming. There were no "canned" programs when we started so we had to do our own programming. Sending persons to programming schools was a necessity. I attended two week-long management seminars sponsored by IBM—one in Endicott, NY and the other in Poughkeepsie, NY. I never learned to program and only knew enough to be dangerous. Our first units rented for $2400 per month. We later upgraded to 16,000 positions of core storage and later to 64,000. Going to random access in retrospect was the obviously right decision. Punch cards quickly became obsolete. Of course you never have enough capacity so keeping the lid on requirements was an opportunity for vigilance. John was the one who kept the explosion under control.

I liked hiring persons with an adequate education but of sterling character. One is not always able to discern character traits with just one interview. Quite often persons were hired on the recommendation of a current employee or someone I knew from the community. Good people can be developed into great people if they have good character. I seldom had to let an individual go because of technical deficiencies but a few had to be let go because they didn't fit in with my perception of the company values. Over time the values of the company began to change but that is later in the story.

We had hired a new receptionist right out of high school and I was visiting with her at the close of work during her first day of work. I was twenty-nine years old, we already had four children but I viewed myself as rather a handsome young guy who wore his years well. During the conversation she asked me how old I was. I asked her to guess. She said, "Oh, I guess you're about forty." I replied, "You just missed it by eleven years!" She replied, "You're not fifty-one, are you?" I think there's a lesson to the story. Anyone who is married with children looks like a middle-aged man to a young girl just out of high school. Other than that she showed reasonably good judgment in her job!

The company was landlocked at its location in downtown Hesston so in 1956 they negotiated for the purchase of ten acres of land on the north side of Dutch Avenue. This was part of a quarter section of land owned by my Uncle Fred and farmed by Uncle Joe. Ray Schlichting negotiated for the purchase of the first ten acres and then subsequently for a larger piece and finally the whole quarter section. Both Uncle Fred and Ray complained to me about the other's intransigence in negotiating. They were both tough negotiators and I just stood on the sidelines and let them "duke" it out.

Ray Schlichting brought a new concept into our accounting system known as *direct costing*. This method of costing put only those costs that varied with the passage of the product through the plant into the value of the product. Costs attributable to passage of time, such as depreciation and other fixed costs were charged to expense rather than added to the value of the inventory. We adopted that method of accounting at Hesston Corporation. Since this was a "cutting edge" concept some of us had the opportunity of presenting this concept at the American Management Association seminars held in Chicago or New York. I had this privilege on a couple occasions in addition to chairing a couple of seminars. The AMA hosted a number of seminars on various management subjects and Hesston Corporation was well represented at these events. Continued education was a hallmark of the decade of the 1960s when the company was growing at a very rapid pace. It was at one of these seminars that I presented what I "modestly" called Hershberger's three laws of control.

Control cannot be exercised after the fact.

For control purposes the part is more important than the total.

Costs accumulate at the point of least pressure

An example of the second law was the decision to cut the travel budget by ten percent. I asked, "Are we going to take fewer trips? Are we going to stay at lower cost hotels? Are we going to eat less expensive meals?" The answer to all these questions was negative—we're just going to cut travel by ten percent. Why does this remind me of the Federal Government? YOU ONLY CONTROL THE TOTAL IF YOU CONTROL THE PARTS THAT MAKE UP THE TOTAL!! There was nothing profound in the statement, just a little common sense which quite often eludes even smart people.

Our family was completed with the arrival of Faith in 1954 and Beth in 1958. Martha had Faith picked out for a girl's name when John, Daniel and Philip came but she finally got to use the name when she had a new daughter. She was named in memory of our oldest child who lived only six months. As Faith was maturing and would soon be entering school Martha was getting concerned about the empty nest and felt that she would like to have another baby. Beth was the answer to that yearning.

We built the house we lived in for the remainder of our years in Hesston, in 1958-59. This house was located on College Drive, just north of the Hesston College campus. We had been given a building permit and Murray Bandy, the mayor, had assured me that we would have water and sewer service by the time it was built. When we started the building process he paid a visit to the site and said, "Oh, I thought you were building one block further east." We had water supplied to us by hooking a garden hose to Harold Dyck's sillcock a block away. Sewer was handled by draining the sewage into perforated field tile. Since the soil was very dense there was very little absorption so drainage was

(Faith and Beth)

kept to a minimum. By the time frost came in 1959 we had both sewer and water service. I had visited the building site after work the evening of November 7, 1958 and stepped on a board with a sixteen penny spike protruding from it with the sharp side up. It went right through my shoe and an inch into the ball of my foot. It was powerfully painful. In the early morning hours of the next day, Beth was born. I had been present at the birth of all the children and wasn't going to miss this one. As I was sitting beside Martha during the birthing process I got a little light headed and I heard a nurse say, "Get his head down between his knees, he's going to pass out on us." It was the only time in my life that I ever came close to fainting, but this time it was close. I recovered and stayed with the birth until Martha named her, Beth Anne. Later that day when four-year-old Faith was asked by someone what the name of her little sister was she said, "Bethlehem."

We usually took a major family trip every summer. This was normally out of state but one summer we used our home as our motel and went out on day trips to various Kansas locations. A memorable vignette was one evening in Pratt, when we stopped for supper. It was a nice café by Kansas standards. As we were waiting for our meal three couples came in very well dressed. The oldest of the men was hosting the group. When they were seated we overheard him say, "I'm going to have a hamburger but please feel free to order anything you want." They all ordered hamburgers!!

Occasionally Martha would accompany me on business trips. She enjoyed the break from family responsibilities and usually we were at a nice hotel and she had all day free to do whatever she wanted to do. I had the evenings free to have a nice dinner with her and take in some good entertainment.

In the summer of 1959 we had the first Brenneman family reunion at Hungry Horse, Montana. My parents and all of my siblings and their families were present except for daughter Beth. It was a memorable time. Although my grandparents weren't living anymore all of the uncles and aunts were there. All of the males slept in a large bunk house and the women in another one. I had three boys with me ages six, seven and eight who needed absolutely no supervision. They

(Brenneman Family reunion – 1961)

were having a wonderful time sleeping with the men and playing with their cousins. I understand the women weren't having quite as much fun as the men. There were lots of stories told and lots of laughing until we played ball, then it got serious. It was the first exposure Martha had to the larger Brenneman family and she was shocked grown men argued like children. It must have been to my credit she hadn't observed that characteristic in me! These reunions have continued ever since at three-year increments.

In 1963 we took a memorable trip to the east coast with our whole family. We stayed with Uncle Paul and Aunt Grace and then one morning drove to New York City to the Worlds Fair. Uncle Paul said I should follow him, which I did. It was a wild and crazy ride. Trying to follow anyone through rush hour traffic is tough but following Uncle Paul was almost impossible. We did not make any friends along the way! After spending the day at the Fair we drove over to New Jersey for supper with both families, fourteen total, and then Paul, Grace, Martha and I went back to New York to see the stage play, *Oliver*. Bill, Paul's eldest, drove the family of children back to Doylestown, PA. I don't believe our actions were very prudent but we all arrived safely back in Doylestown in due time with only my billfold suffering from the indiscretion.

In 1957 my father suffered his first stroke. He was to preach on Sunday morning but my mother noticed he was slurring his words and called me to find out if I could take him to the doctor.

(Our house on College Drive – 1962)

She then called Roy Roth, president of Hesston College, and asked him if he could preach. He consented and I took my father to the emergency room at Bethel Hospital with my mother. Dr. Preheim saw him and diagnosed him with a mild stroke. Dad had a history of high blood pressure that was difficult to control with the medications available. In the evening I stayed with him while the rest of the family went to church. It suddenly came upon me I would probably never be able to talk to him man to man again. A sense of loss overwhelmed me. Even though I was a man making my own way I still liked to visit with my dad. Though he was able to function well enough to return to work at the Hesston Corporation parts department, he was kept on primarily because he was an employee they valued for past performance and not for current productivity. Mother, with my siblings and I, eventually decided that he should discontinue work.

(Mother, Dad, Uncle Ed and Dr. H)

Five years later Mother and Dad took a train trip to the west coast and up into British Columbia then across to Edmonton on the way to Tofield to visit her sister and other friends. When they boarded the train in Edmonton Mother noticed Dad was not doing well but soon after boarding they noticed he was failing. During the short journey to Tofield the train crew had called ahead to Tofield and an ambulance was waiting to take him to the hospital when they arrived. Mother called us children immediately. The prognosis was not good—the doctors felt he would not survive. I immediately made plans to fly to Edmonton. We had a company plane, a twin engine Beechcraft Baron, scheduled to take a service trip to Spokane, WA and there was room for another passenger. I rode with the service crew. We hit severe turbulence along the front range of the Rockies and I was severely air sick. One of the other passengers also got sick and we could only find one sick sack which we passed back and forth between us. When we got to Spokane we let the service men off and the pilot then flew me to Edmonton. We flew over the top of the Canadian Rockies in the late evening. It was a cloudless night and the air was as smooth as glass. As I looked out the right side of the plane I could see Turner Valley, where there was a perpetual flame from burning waste gas, and beyond to High River, as well as the lights in the rural area where we lived at Mazeppa. It was a poignant moment for me.

Dad survived the stroke but was unable to communicate until his death a year later. Hesston Corporation sent a plane back to Edmonton along with a good friend, Dr. George Hostetler, to pick Dad and Mother up and transport them back to Newton. Hesston Corporation was a very openhanded member of the community. Dad and Mother were not the only persons they airlifted as a generous act of kindness. There was not a good place to keep Dad in his final days. Lloyd and Pearl had a hospital bed and he and mom stayed with them for a short time and then he was moved to Meadowlark Home in Newton for a while. This was not a good facility for him. Finally Schowalter Villa, just being built, was able to take him in the late fall in 1961. He passed away in April of 1962 just short of his sixty-fifth birthday. He was a simple and honorable man whom I loved and respected deeply.

Mother continued to live in her home on South Main for some time and then took a unit for independent living at Schowalter Villa. They had to put an extra window in the unit to allow her to look down the street. Mother liked to see out— it did not bother her that persons could also look in. She lived there until her death in 1979.

(Church in the country)

In the early 1960s the Pennsylvania Mennonite Church, where we worshipped, was facing some decisions. We were not outgrowing our facility but it needed renovation. Running water and indoor plumbing seemed to be a necessity. With that question looming we wondered if we should stay at our rural location, three miles southeast of Hesston. After a good deal of discerning and recognizing our congregation was no longer primarily agrarian the decision was made to move to Hesston. We procured a tract of land on the north side of town, a half mile east of Hesston Corporation and started building in 1963. Ivan Diller, Lois's brother, was the builder. Members of the congregation, as they were able, invested time and material in the project.

An innovative plan for fund raising was employed. The persons appointed to the finance committee each made their own pledge commitment before they asked the next person to make a pledge. In this manner everyone had made their own pledge before they asked the next person. A suggested level of giving was two dollars per week for every $1000 of salary. We were able to secure most of the total in five-year pledges before construction began. The total building cost was just over $100,000. Martha and I were able to pledge $10,000, a new mark for us. From a congregation of seventy-five we were able to build a facility that would seat 250-275.

Being on the building committee required a good amount of time—usually evening hours. The design was unique for the time and it featured a high white rock front that was quite prominent as one approached the church. There was considerable discussion about naming the church—should we retain our old name or use a new one indicating new beginnings. At a meeting when the discussion took place Mother Hershberger referred to the passage in Revelation 2:17 "to him that overcometh will I give to eat of the hidden manna, and will give him a white stone, and in the stone a new name written, which no man knoweth saving he that receiveth it." That verse capped the decision that the name would be *Whitestone*.

The first Sunday we moved to town a number of new families started attending. Most of them were from General Conference Mennonite background. They quickly became assimilated into the congregation and although they were never solicited they contributed generously toward the building until we were debt free.

Donald King was our pastor in those early years. He was the first fully-supported pastor we had, replacing Martha's father. After my father's death we had only a single pastor. I was chair of the church when the time came for a performance review for pastor King. We had been working with him, along with conference overseer, Howard Zehr, to help him in his sermon presentation and delivery. Although Donald was seminary trained he was not a strong pulpit man. The council and the overseer, sensing the feeling of the congregation, believed we needed a change but Donald felt we were misreading the congregation. He asked for a vote and received either slightly more or slightly less than a fifty percent vote for continuation. It was devastating for him. I was strongly blamed by him and his wife for not giving proper leadership and rallying the congregation behind him. It was one of life's difficult lessons for me and for him. He resigned immediately. We needed to find an interim pastor after his resignation.

John Friesen was a long-term missionary to India. He was coming home on furlough and was planning on being in the Hesston community during most of a year beginning in 1966. He was returning from India through Africa where his son was serving as a missionary. I wrote to him in Africa asking him if he would serve as interim pastor. I did not hear from him but when he arrived at Whitestone

(Whitestone Mennonite Church – 1964)

we gave him a royal welcome and he accepted the position. He humbly and genuinely was a servant leader. About a month after he started I received his letter from Africa declining to serve! When I showed him the letter he laughed, "When you gave me such a warm reception I didn't have the heart to turn you down." The Lord had delayed the mail, I believe.

Jerry Weaver, son of India missionaries Ed and Irene Weaver, then became our pastor. It was a time of growth and excitement. During the school year attendance was 400 to 450 as many students joined in the celebrative services. My term as church chair expired soon after Jerry came although I was chair of the congregation again when Paul Brunner came in 1975.

In April of 1965 we had another major event. Martha had noticed a lump in her left breast and went to her primary care physician, Dr. Wilmer Harms. After examining her he recommended that she have a biopsy to determine the nature of the lump. Our Sunday school class brought in food when she was hospitalized. Velma Swartzendruber had brought in a special casserole dish. Just before we sat down to eat I received word from the doctor the lump was malignant and they recommended a radical mastectomy to be performed on Monday morning. I sat back down to the table and inhaled the food—I have no recollection of eating or chewing. Immediately after gulping down the food I left for Newton, with a horrendous stomach ache, to be with Martha. We wept and prayed together. She immediately thought of *breast*; I immediately thought of *cancer*. Dr. Myers, a Newton surgeon, performed the surgery on Monday. After sending the surrounding lymph nodes in they didn't discover any lymph node involvement but they recommended radiation therapy. They needed to do some skin grafting later, taking skin from her abdomen to graft to the area where they had removed the breast. This was a very painful and distressing experience for Martha. How would I feel, was a question I had. I had already decided in my head but would my emotion follow my head? It did. Martha was still the beautiful woman she always had been, scarred, yes, beautiful YES! She was thirty-eight years old at the time and has now been cancer free for forty-six years! Praise the Lord! Two years later she had a hysterectomy.

(Phil, John, Me, Faith, Martha, Beth, Dan – 1964)

About once a year I would come home "sick" on a Friday evening and would immediately go to bed with a couple books. Martha and the children let me alone except for a minimum amount of nourishment and I would get up on Monday morning ready to go to work again. I never went to the doctor for these "illnesses" but they seemed real enough at the time. It probably was a relief valve that kept me from blowing up the following week. During the early 1960s the two oldest boys had the paper route for the Wichita Eagle in Hesston. When they inquired about taking this responsibility I told them that it was going to be *their* paper route, neither mine nor their mother's. We had some friends that had a son with the paper route in his name but the parents did all the work. The boys were responsible for waking themselves up, taking the route, and doing the collecting at the end of the month. I'm not sure how long they had it but they were very responsible and except for stormy weather covered the town with the Wichita Eagle on their bicycles.

In 1967 Roy Mullet, president of Excel Industries, asked me if I would consider coming over to Excel Industries as their chief financial officer. He caught me at a time when I was a bit frustrated with my position at Hesston Corporation. After hearing his offer I told him I would need a little time to reflect on it but I thought it was an attractive and fair offer. Ray Schlichting, however, was gone at that time and I told Roy I couldn't give him a response until after Ray returned and I had a chance to talk to him. My memory of what Ray said was something to this effect, "You're not leaving so let's talk about what can be changed to satisfy you."

Hesston Corporation had an operating committee which met weekly. Lyle Yost chaired those meetings and Ray kept the minutes. This was the chief decision-making group for the operating decisions of the company. I was not a member of this group at the time and was not until some years later, when Howard Brenneman became president. The company decided to set up a steering committee which was to implement the decisions made by the operating committee, to put the wheels on the wagon. As chair of the steering committee I met with them as a non-voting member to be in on the ground floor of decisions made. The package Ray presented was the setting up of the steering committee, which I was to chair, a nice salary increase and a company car. I decided to stick it out!

(Mother with children and grandchildren – 1967 – seeing if we're all in line!)

The operating committee meetings were not without conflict. They battled out decisions in a very spirited manner. One time, Ray Adee, the chief engineer, came out of one of the meetings and said of a certain decision, "It barely passed; six of us were against it and Lyle was for it." Lyle wouldn't nor couldn't have been that dominant but it was a humorous look at the activities of the committee.

In the summer of 1967 we took our last big family trip with all of the members of our family. We were gone for 3 weeks, traveling to the west coast via the southern route and back through the central area. I booked all of the motel accommodations in advance. We had a budget of fifty dollars per day exclusive of gas. We lived within the budget! John was a junior in high school that year and enjoyed going off to do his own thing and getting lost. When we were in Los Angeles we were at the Compton Relays and were able to see Jim Ryun break the world record for the mile. This time Dan wasn't with us. They were having a motorcycle show on the same grounds as the relays and he had opted to go to that since he was into motorcycles at the time. A traumatic event happened in San Francisco China town. Martha had to take Beth to the bathroom and I also needed to go and we left Faith with the boys instructing them to stay right where they were until we returned. When I returned Faith was not there. The boys decided they wanted to see something else and had left Faith with the instructions to stay right there until they returned. When they returned she was gone. We had parked on the street about a half mile from where we left her. It was not straight down the street but several zigzags from where we were. We walked on both sides of the street looking into the stores until we finally reached the car. She was not there. Martha stayed with the car while the boys and I retraced our steps and again returned to the car. She was standing calmly with Martha by the car as if nothing had happened. We praised the Lord that nothing had!

When we returned from the trip Martha and I were standing by the kitchen sink and it was nice and quiet. Martha said, "They're all here and I can't see one of them." Togetherness was wonderful but getting a little space was wonderful also!

In the spring of 1973 we attended three graduation exercises for our children and should have attended four but could not be two places at once. Dan graduated from EMC, Phil from Hesston College, Faith from Hesston High and Beth from Hesston Grade School. We were unable to be at Phil's. I guess it was too close; it also was on the same day that Dan graduated in Virginia. These were also some turbulent years for us and our children. I will leave it for them to tell their own stories.

(The Buckwalter family – 1963)

The hippie movement had its effect on our children and so also on us. Their struggles in coming to faith and having their faith tested were, of course, unique to each of them. We felt they needed to pay most of their own college tuition costs and we would help as needed so they could graduate from college without debt. They all did except for Beth who decided against completing college. John and Dan worked on bridge construction for King Construction during the summer months and earned very good money for long hours and heavy lifting. Faith, always competitive, was upset girls couldn't earn the money boys did. I suggested she apply to Hesston Corporation for a summer job. One of her interests was secretarial work so she applied. They told her they did not have a secretarial opening but did have an opening for a welder on the second shift. She took it and surprised her mother with the announcement. She turned out to be a very good welder. Her supervisor did not know she was my daughter until she left at the end of the summer. My stock went up several points in the eyes of the foreman! Her income exceeded her brothers that summer!

Beginning in the late 1960s and the 1970s I traveled to Europe numerous times. We had exported our products to Europe but in the late 1960s we opened a plant in Udine, Italy. It was a small plant in northern Italy and was quite difficult to get to. I opined on an occasion or two that getting there was difficult enough to believe that your assignment was complete when you made the scene. The fact was that the assignment had only begun. Martha was of the opinion that snow storms, stopped up sewers and air conditioning going out always waited to happen until I left for Europe and completely out of reach. It did seem that way.

(With Mel Blosser at Udine, Italy)

One time, when I was scheduled to leave for Europe, we received word that son John was involved in a serious accident close to Souderton, PA and was taken to the ICU of a Philadelphia hospital. He had completely crushed his VW bug and they had to use "the jaws of life" to get him out of the car. I re-routed my flight through Philadelphia and visited him in the ICU. By this time he was out of immediate danger but they were continuing to monitor him. After he got out of the hospital he stayed with Uncle Paul and Aunt Grace in Doylestown to mend for a couple weeks. When he was recovered he returned to Hesston and shortly started working at the Schowalter Villa in the kitchen for Elizabeth Barge. He discovered a lot of neat old men there and they took a fancy to him. Having a man in the kitchen was particularly important to them.

Later the company set up European operations in Brussels, a parts warehouse in Paris and another manufacturing facility in Coex, France. A rather typical reaction when setting up systems and procedures in another country was for them to say, "No problem, no problem" and when I would return a month or two later they would say, "It's not possible, It's not possible!" The first was a ruse to get me off their back and out the door. The reason it was not possible, when I returned, was because the law did not allow them to make that kind of change. It usually wasn't against the law as far as I could determine but it did keep me on the defensive so I wasn't so offensive! By the mid-1970s we had a European Operations controller stationed in Hesston so he had the primary responsibility but I still thought it was necessary to make the scene on many occasions.

During the late 1960s to mid 1970s we were acquiring a lot of new companies. Most of them were small and many of them were unprofitable when we acquired them. I was involved in most of the acquisitions and it was a wonderful education. Later after they were acquired I would visit them at the end of each month to review their financial results. This took me out of town a lot of the time. For some of the earlier acquisitions I would fly commercial which would require that I be gone overnight but later we had our own jets to make those trips. When the aircraft manufacturers are making their pitch for corporate jets they point out you can take additional persons who should also be included but the cost of sending multiple persons commercially could be too pricey. The problem with the multiple seats available on your own jet is they get filled with persons who really don't need to go but do because space is available. As a result of this problem these small to medium-sized companies got visits from corporate headquarters by every operating department. This caused a lot of work for the subsidiaries in preparing for the visit and hosting them every month. The jets were wonderful—wheels up at seven with breakfast on board and return by six or seven and home for the night. I need to say that when the company was much smaller and we had two company planes, one a single engine and one a twin engine I said, "Lyle has just one bad habit, that's airplanes, but we can afford it." Later when we had two Cessna Citation jets I intoned, "Lyle has just one bad habit, that's airplanes, and we *can't* afford it."

In 1974 the organization was changed to set up a separate corporate entity. A new corporate office building was added which was "state of the art." It was a beautiful structure and housed most of the corporate staff that at the time of my departure in 1976 numbered ninety persons. After the establishment of the corporate headquarters I no longer had the control responsibility for the Hesston Manufacturing facility since I now had the control oversight of all the operating units. I had a staff of five plus a secretary, rather than the much larger group I supervised before the establishment of the corporate group. In harkening back to my beginning years when all of the accounting personnel were in one small, low-ceilinged room, the persons reporting to me were at least an eighth of a mile from my office, except for my secretary. My office was on the second floor so in order for my staff to contact me they would call to see if I was available and then walk an eighth of a mile to my office or talk on the phone. Communication had become more complicated. I had a beautiful, well-appointed office. We had flown to Chicago to pick out our furnishings—each person had a budget of $5000 which was half the price of a new luxury car at that time. It *appeared* everything was going well!

Howard Brenneman, my namesake and first cousin, became president in 1974. I had hired him in accounting right after he graduated from high school and married in 1959. He was a quick learner but I counseled him that he would need to get a college education if he was going to succeed in the corporate world. I told him that he could work as much as he wanted to during his college years. I believe he worked at least 30 hours a week all during those years and full time during the summer. After graduating from college he had various positions in accounting and then transferred to marketing and corporate planning. In 1974, with his ascendancy to the presidency, he set up his own organization and I was appointed vice-president reporting directly to him rather than Ray. There was a group of senior vice-presidents that functioned more in an advisory role and spent more of their time pursuing other interests. The additional overhead put in place was starting to take its toll. Most of the persons now on the operating committee with me were closer to Howard's age—I was a senior member and probably too conservative. The role of the operating committee had changed substantially because we were now responsible for all of the operating divisions, not just the Hesston plant.

The company had gone public in 1968 and the stock was sold over the counter. In 1973, with a good deal of fanfare the stock was listed as

HES on the New York Stock Exchange. We were in the big leagues! The initial public offering came off very smoothly and the stock made a nice move after the event. When we were listed on the NYSE it was a whole new world with a lot of new pressures. Every quarter had to be better than the previous one or the prior year quarter. Sales growth was pegged at twenty percent annually which had been quite doable when we were a twenty million dollar company but was a giant leap at two-hundred million. These sales had to be achieved either through acquisitions, new product sales or increases in our current lines. The pressure was on and the investors in the stock needed to be satisfied. We had a brand new group of owners to keep happy.

A policy among farm equipment manufacturers was to carry the cost of dealer inventory for them. The dealers enjoyed this and it allowed them to have a good selection of products without needing to pay the interest on the money. There was a due date to be met but it was far enough down the road they weren't always worried enough. With the downturn in the farm economy and the pressure for more and more sales, life was a pressure cooker in the corporate tower, fondly known as the Taj Mahal or the Taj for short.

We were negotiating with Versatile Manufacturing in Winnipeg concerning an acquisition of their company in 1976. Howard B. and Dick Hrdlicka, our corporate attorney, had made the initial contact and two weeks later I accompanied them for a return visit. They had recounted when the corporate jet landed at Grand Forks, ND to clear customs, they decided they were both born in Newton, KS because they had no passports with them. Dick was born in Czechoslovakia and Howard in Alberta. I told Howard I never had any problem telling border officials the truth so he decided he would get it straight this time through. Howard was following me and suddenly he moved in front of me and told the official he was born in Newton. I told the official I was born in Alberta and he waved me through. When I caught up with Howard I inquired about the change. "This is a small airport and I saw it was the same official I told I was born in Newton and he might have remembered it." If you always tell the truth you don't have to have a good memory.

We needed to go for a secondary public offering in 1976. We spent a whole day going over the prospectus in New York with the lawyers and the accountants and then to the bar where I nursed a 7-Up for two hours waiting for dinner. The objective in the exercise with the lawyers and the accountants, in my judgment, was not to make the prospectus clearer for the casual reader but to make it look as good as possible and still not get sued if it didn't turn out as good as we hoped it would. When I retired to my room for the night I had a direct word from the Lord, "What is a poor farm boy like you doing here?" I didn't have an answer—I was going to need to make a change.

Later that fall, Howard Brenneman stopped by my office shortly after 5:00. I had a meeting going on but he stepped in and asked if I could see him in his office at 7:30 the next morning. It was not an unusual request and I told him it would be fine and I'd be there.

That night the Lord woke me up just after midnight and told me what Howard wanted to talk to me about. I was angry at first and then calmed down and went over in my mind how I was going to respond. The revelation was in great detail so I had worked out my response in the same detail. About five o'clock I woke up Martha and said, "Let's go out for breakfast, I have something to share with you." We went out for breakfast and I explained what I thought I needed to do.

At 7:30 I went into Howard's office, he closed the door and after a few pleasantries told me he was going to need to make some changes in the corporate structure. He was going to appoint a CFO and it would be either me or Mel Voth, who was serving as treasurer. If I chose to stay on as controller I would still have the title of vice-president but would no longer be on the operating committee. I responded, "I don't want the position of CFO, even if offered. Mel wants it very badly, so all we need to discuss is severance since I will not report to Mel Voth." I didn't feel that Howard had been completely forthcoming with me in saying that he was going to choose one of us. Yes, he was going to choose one of us but I already knew who that was. He wanted me to stay on for a couple months so there would be an orderly transition and he wanted me to make another trip to Italy. After a little more discussion he called in John Siemens, director of personnel, to discuss my severance package. I already had that in mind and they agreed to it and I was *Free At Last!* Fellow employees felt I was a "Lifer" and were shocked I had resigned. All kinds of people came and in the melee I forgot to call my lover, Martha, who was privately stewing at home.

I did not hold any animus toward Howard B. He had a tough job and was under an enormous amount of pressure. He had been given a mandate and was doing all he could to achieve it. I was not a good fit for his inner circle and I think he was relieved that I decided to move on. We have continued to be good friends.

In the next couple months I discovered something I was only peripherally aware of. I was no longer in a position of power so the political folks were already deciding which way the wind would blow and who would hold the hoops they needed to jump through. The majority, however, continued to interact with me as if nothing had changed. I was particularly gratified a number of marketing people, whom I regularly did battle with, continued to seek my counsel.

Martha had a much more difficult time adjusting to my changed status. I was unemployed! I thought it was freeing, she wondered what this held for her and for our family. I did very little to alleviate her fears. I was looking at all kinds of possibilities.

Shortly after my resignation, Jim Crumpler, senior auditor for Arthur Young, took Martha and me to dinner in Wichita. It was a long dinner and when we got home Martha said, "Now I understand why you needed to leave." Being a part of the conversation of the inner workings of the corporation helped her to appreciate the subtleties I was unable to articulate previously.

(Faith, Beth and Martha in the Alps)

Lyle was the only one that seemed to feel a little betrayed. I was a long-term employee whom he had hired fresh out of college with no training in accounting and had become a trusted and valued employee. He didn't understand why I thought I needed to leave. It helped that later I went to work for Hesston College, a favorite institution for him.

One of the heady potions that we all drank of at Hesston Corporation is, we could be successful no matter what we put our hand to. Of course it wasn't true but it was part of the culture that allowed many of the personnel to leave Hesston Corporation and secure good positions or begin their own enterprise.

Howard B. had wanted me to return to Italy one more time and I convinced him that the company should pay for Martha, Faith and Beth to accompany me. We had a wonderful and relaxing time at a resort along the Adriatic Sea. Martha and the girls had the day to themselves while I went to work. In the evening we would have a nice dinner out and spend the evening on our balcony overlooking the sea.

I think it was the evening of my resignation that we met with our small group from Whitestone. When they found out I resigned there was unbridled rejoicing for the decision. Martha felt the affirmation was so strong it seemed a repudiation of the validity of my employment there. Martha is more sensitive than me about such matters so she probably was right.

I had served on the Board of Overseers of Hesston College for six years, most of that time as chairman so I became well acquainted with their operations. I was on the search committee that found Laban Peachey to succeed Tilman Smith as president. After my term was over on the overseer board I became a member again of The Mennonite Board of Education which oversaw the colleges of the Mennonite Church. I was treasurer of the board which was mostly a name appointment, I think. Could it be I was supposed to be doing something I was unaware of?

Laban was up for re-appointment as president but there was some question about it because he had a different way of reasoning than the executive secretary of the board of education had. I describe it as circular rather than linear. Accountants mostly think in a linear fashion. Laban's reasoning was sometimes outside the box. Laban had asked me to join the team at the college very shortly after I resigned at the corporation but I was unsure about moving that direction. It was a good fall-back position but I was uncertain if it was the right direction for me. The Mennonite Board of Education strongly encouraged me to join his team. Since I was a linear thinker working closely with Laban I could help interpret him to them. Laban was appointed to another term and had a very successful presidency.

The last year of my tenure at Hesston Corporation was their last profitable year for some years into the future. It certainly was not because I left, but I saw the handwriting on the wall and I felt powerless to make any difference. There have been many persons who have expounded on the reasons for the rise and fall of Hesston Corporation so I will not add my voice to the chorus.

I was the first in a long line of persons who left or were terminated by Hesston in the following years. Getting ahead of the curve was important in terms of severance package as well as leaving with a mutually-good feeling. I have wondered since, if the Lord hadn't awakened me at midnight would the results have been different? Two years after I left, the company sold fifty percent ownership to Fiat of Italy.

I had some questions when leaving Hesston Corp. What is a poor farm boy doing in the corporate tower? What will be the next step and can I handle it? Is there life after Hesston Corp? Since I look like a "success" why don't I feel like one?

Musings on my Hesston Corporation years

In writing the story of Hesston Corporation it seems like an unusual story and I was part of it. When I left I commented I would not have hired anyone with my qualifications, or lack thereof, for any position I was responsible for. Lyle gave me an opportunity and I'm indebted to him for it. Through it all I see the Lord's hand leading out of medicine and into Hesston Corporation and out again. I had wonderful co-workers and mentors to whom I will always be indebted.

A book I have read recently *The Speed of Trust* by Stephen Covey, seems particularly cogent. When you trust the other party or person with whom you are dealing things work or move quickly. When you don't trust it takes a long time and often lawyers are involved on both sides to try to overcome the mistrust with enforceable legal provisions. I certainly noticed this in the many acquisitions we were involved in at Hesston Corporation. On the personal side I reported to Ray Schlichting for twenty-plus of the twenty-five years I worked there. I had complete trust and respect for his integrity. He was not without his faults, no one is, but he never overrode my decisions or went behind my back. I could safely tell the people who worked for me, if they had problems they didn't feel comfortable talking to me about, they were free to talk to Ray. If someone came to Ray with a problem that needed to be addressed to me he invariably would ask, "Have you talked to Howard about it?" This trust relationship was a wonderful example to me then and in later years. I would never work, on a long-term basis, for someone I didn't both trust and respect.

I left with a strong pro-business bias. Most companies we dealt with were honest, upright corporate citizens who could be trusted to do the right thing. There were exceptions but they seemed rare to me.

Martha and our children stood by me through it all and put up with my frequent absences when they could have used me at home. During this period all of our children, except John, were born and by the time I left only Faith and Beth were still in college. Daniel and Philip had married during these years. As John once said when he was in the early grades, "When my dad grows up he's going to be a farmer like Uncle Lloyd."

I presume I was on a *power trip* and was almost completely unaware of it. The reaction of our small group when I resigned gave me a hint of this. I hardly recognize the person I write about during these years. It seems like such a different life than I would have envisioned for myself. The kid growing up in Tofield and Mazeppa is more easily identifiable to me now than the corporate executive.

Those were wonderful years in which I learned a great deal but had a great deal still to learn.

Hesston College Administration years (1976-81)

I joked that the difference between working at Hesston Corporation and Hesston College was I went out the front door to go to the corporation and out the back door to go to the college. (We lived on the edge of campus with our back door facing the campus.) There was a quantum difference in terms of my work assignment. There were some, who didn't know me very well, who thought I was going to retire when I left the corporation. If they thought being in charge of development at a private church-related college was retirement they needed to have their heads examined! A very basic difference between the jobs was that at the corporation my phone rang with people wanting to talk with me. Suddenly no one *wanted* to talk to me; I *wanted* to talk to them! This was a marketing job that I had some concept of but very little experience. I needed to take the initiative in a new way. My salary was about a third of what it had been at the corporation. It was nice that we had no house mortgage or consumer debt! A large mortgage or other debt load would have precluded us from making this move.

I probably thought, in more than a peripheral way, I would join Laban's team at Hesston College as I resigned at Hesston Corporation. Laban had approached me before I was sure I would leave the corporation. I was brought on as Director of Finance. This included the business office, maintenance, food services and fund raising. They had a good group already in place in all of these areas, except fund raising so a great deal of my time and energy went into raising funds. The college was on good financial footing so there was no pressing need to make changes to that area of the operations.

I was part of the administrative cabinet and was looked on a little askance by some on the cabinet. One time when Laban was gone, John Lederach took me on by saying "We don't need anyone here as a stooge for the Mennonite Board of Education." He was of the opinion that I had been placed in my position at the behest of them rather than Laban. I informed him Laban had hired me just like he had hired him and I assured him I was not a "stooge" for the Board of Education. Over time he became convinced it was true and we became good friends and colleagues.

Shortly after beginning at the college I was asked to be a "businessman in residence" at The Associated Mennonite Biblical Seminary in Elkhart, IN. It was there I met Milo Shantz, from Ontario, who was also in the same program. We were at the seminary for a week and went to classes with the students. I was asked to give the chapel address on Thursday of the week we were there. Milo, who cast a much longer financial shadow than I, opted out of that assignment. I had the choice of either giving my life story or some theological treatise. Many years later when visiting at the seminary the business manager told me he remembered something I said at that chapel! What I had said was "Accounting for a church related institution is no more *holy work* than accounting for a secular institution." The difference was some persons who worked at church institutions felt they didn't need personal spiritual nourishment because they were at a church institution. Both needed the larger church and regular nourishment. Apparently it struck a chord with him.

Another incident from that stay was in a class taught by John Howard Yoder, the Mennonite guru and theologian. He asked Milo how he kept from being overly influential in the church for his own purposes because of his wealth. Joe Hertzler, the development officer of the seminary, put the question right back to John Howard, "How do you keep from being overly influential in the church for your own purposes because of your superior intellect and teaching and preaching ability?" I didn't believe John Howard had a good answer for that. Whatever our gifts they need to be dedicated to the God who gave them because great gifts have great power.

Milo Shantz and I were good friends until the day of his death. The last time I met him at a MEDA convention he was heavily invested in the political campaign of a Canadian individual who was running for prime minister, I believe. I thought there could be more worthwhile endeavors but I could have been wrong. It was his calling, not mine.

These were very heady years for Hesston College with enrollment reaching record levels, so the annual fund was not under as much pressure as it was later when enrollment declined. One of the first things we instituted was a program we labeled "Partners" for those who contributed $1000 or more annually to the operating fund. The year before I came there were only fifteen persons who had contributed at that level. This became a top priority. Bill Mason, Director of Student Services, and with a lot of marketing experience, was very helpful in designing the program. I believe we increased the number of partners to seventy-five during my first year.

Laban was a wonderful friend and stimulator. His office was right next door and we did a lot of planning together concerning persons we needed to contact. We spent a lot of time traveling together raising funds for the college. He was relentlessly optimistic. One time in Iowa, after visiting a wealthy farmer who treated us rather shabbily, Laban commented as we drove away, "I think in his heart of hearts he would really like to help us." I saw no evidence of that! He was also not a very attentive driver. There were so many more important things to observe and comment on than driving a car down the road between two lines on the pavement.

His mind was constantly at work in creating new ideas for the college. One often quoted was "If I want to find out what the college should be doing, I don't talk to the educators, I talk to the farmers." Another like comment, "God first talked to man in the garden and it still is the place where God meets man." It could be that such comments made the Board of Education look a bit askance at their lead educator in Hesston.

In 1976, Martha and I took her father Earl to Iowa for the funeral of his sister-in-law. He had wanted very badly to drive up by himself but he did not have good eyesight and the doctor recommended he only drive locally. We should have had a tape recorder! He talked non-stop, except while eating, all the way up and all the way back. He recounted many interesting stories of his long life and times of long ago. He was a gifted storyteller. He had gone by car to California with three of his brothers at the death of his oldest brother Sam. He returned home bummed out because his brothers Paul and Frank had completely dominated the conversation with all of their stories. We surmised that he was unable to tell his own!

The year 1977 brought serious distress to Martha. In March her sister Alice died after a long bout with cancer. Particularly distressing to Martha was that she was not able to tell her goodbye. She talked to Alice the morning of her death and Alice still felt she was going to be healed. She was a very stalwart and committed Christian. We attended her funeral in Scottdale, PA. In April, a month later, Martha's mother died after some years of having strokes that affected her thinking and emotions but she was still able to function in a limited way. She was in assisted living at the Villa with Dad Earl. A strong woman of faith, we rejoiced that she could be released.

That summer Dad Earl began noticing one of his contemporaries, Keturah Dreier. That summer he went to Puerto Rico visiting Martha's sister Esther Rose and husband. Esther was a bit put off by his seeming infatuation with this new love of his life. In October he married Keturah. His son Albert, on furlough from Argentina, performed the ceremony. Seven weeks later he suffered a severe stroke, lapsed into a deep coma, and died two weeks later. A memorable event was Ralph, Genny, and Michael, just returning from Japan, standing by his bedside singing "A Gentle Hallelujah" at ten in the evening. The song is based on Hosea 6:1. A very touching moment!

Losing three family members within one year and getting a new stepmother overloaded Martha's circuits rather severely. She was the executor of his modest estate that included two large Indian and Harley-Davidson motorcycles he was restoring. She had been the one that *had stayed with the stuff* while her siblings had gone all over the world so she had a special relationship with her parents. The transition with her dad was particularly difficult; he had been her father, her minister and mentor. In later years, particularly as he courted and then married Keturah, she was his confidant. It was a period of disquiet for Martha.

I had been in Montana visiting on behalf of the college and had stayed at my Cousin Katherine Lapp's home. She baked delicious bread from wheat that she had ground with a small stone mill grinder. This seemed like a good possibility for a business so when I returned to Hesston I mentioned it to John. He was intrigued by the possibility. Bob Razook had a corner lot just south of the business district in Hesston he wanted to sell. John heard about it and wondered if we would help him buy it. He bought the house with the thought the small building in the back could be used as a bakery. He quickly abandoned that idea and built a block building with a full basement right next to his house. The lower level had an outside entrance from the front and Paul Friesen used it as an art studio during the time John had the bakery.

John had baked a couple loaves of bread but nothing mass produced. He was of the opinion that baking in large quantities was different enough so baking in small batches first would not be helpful. The first day his bakery opened he baked LOTS more bread than he had produced in his whole life previously. The results were a bit mixed the first day but he soon had the process down. He quickly had a strong *cult* following plus those who just liked good homemade bread. It was a year or two before he could be convinced to bake cinnamon rolls. They had too much sugar for the true believers. His cinnamon rolls were soon very well received.

Travel was much different than it had been with the corporation. I sometimes stayed in homes to save travel expense. One of the first trips I took to Colorado Martha went with me. We stayed in a small motel in La Junta but I was delayed on a contact I was making. Martha got evicted from her room in mid morning and was sitting on a chair in a very small lobby with our luggage, waiting on me when I returned late noon. On the way home Martha said "I've supported you in your decision to do this but just don't take me along." I almost totally followed that advice in the ensuing five years that I was at the college. When traveling for the corporation I almost always had the evenings free. Traveling for the college, evenings were "prime time" for making calls and arranging for the next day schedule—not particularly conducive for fun and games.

Sometime after this incident Faith called from Goshen College and said "Well, Dad, how is life in the cold, cruel world of the Christian corporation?" I occasionally would use the term "the cold, cruel corporate world" in making light of the vagaries of the business world. Her allusions to the college world were interesting because it made me realize that life was very similar in many respects in both worlds. There was still some dissonance between the faculty and administration, not dissimilar between management and labor in the business world. When coming into the college world I always equated the faculty with "management." When I set up the first budget after arriving I realized they considered themselves, similar to labor from my background, as pawns in the game being played by the administration. They did not consider staff or administration one of them. To me there still seemed to be a "pecking order" in place. Another practice that I noticed was how terminations were handled. The corporate world was in many ways kinder than the "Christian corporation." In the world I came from if a person was not working out they were terminated with proper severance and often helped to find another position. The college in an attempt to be more redemptive put up with marginal competence but kept the employee employed. Almost always the incompetence was recognized and the employee was subtly marginalized.

I am probably being too hard on the college with the above characterization but it needs to be recognized that people have warts no matter where they work and finding a good fit is a concern for secular and sacred alike. Christian institutions are not an exception. The moral, spiritual and ethical standards of my comrades at the college, as a whole, were certainly higher than I experienced in corporate life.

Even though the college was operating at capacity, or somewhat above capacity, there was still a short-fall from tuition revenue to balance the budget. During this time individual churches were moving away from giving major support from their offerings or budgets to the church institutions and more and more of the institutions needed to add their own development staff. This has continued unabated since I left the college almost thirty years ago. As enrollment declined later it took more contributed dollars to balance the operating budget. It is just as important for our church institutions to be operating at capacity as it is in the business world. The purpose of the college is not to raise funds but to educate students so a *first* priority is to fill our dorms with dues-paying students. Student recruitment is more important than fund raising particularly if the college has idle capacity.

The dilemma facing the not-for-profit institutions is that too many of the contributed dollars have to be used for the fund raising effort. I was a part-time fund raiser when I started at the college. I added an associate, Loren Kremer, the year before I left and spent full time on it myself the last year when we were raising funds for the Yost Center. In 2010 the development staff needs to raise much more and so needs more staff.

I was at a meeting at the Colonial House when I received a call that my mother had fallen in her front yard and an ambulance had taken her to Bethel Hospital. I immediately went to her home and found out she had in all likelihood died before the ambulance came. They were a little perplexed that she was wearing two dresses when she died. She had dressed up to go to a funeral but had decided to shake out a few flour sacks that she was going to wash and hem for dish towels. In order not to soil her good dress it was assumed that she had put an old dress over top the good one. She died as she lived—busy living life with devotion to duty and frugality. Although I loved my mother we didn't always have a smooth relationship.

She wanted more from me, I felt, than I was able or willing to give. We didn't argue but there was often tension. She was wonderfully supportive when we had difficulties and completely accepting of our children and her other grandchildren. In writing this story of my life I gained a new appreciation for her and the sacrifices that she needed to make, particularly in the Alberta years. She was a good though forceful Mennonite mother who loved us all dearly. We would not have made it to Hesston without her. She was seventy-eight years old when she passed away.

We siblings, Lois (Glenn's widow), Pearl, James, John and I, with our spouses, had a joyous time of remembering as we divided her things after her passing. The items were divided into groups of comparable things and the oldest got to choose first on the first lot. On the second lot, the second sibling got to choose first, etc. We did a lot of kidding as we went through the process—absolutely no feelings someone got something that was rightfully yours.

Other changes occurred in our families. Martha's brother Ralph died after a battle with melanoma at the age of fifty-six. They had returned from Japan for treatment of his cancer and were living in Pasadena. We went out to visit them before he died and I took him to the Los Angeles County General Hospital for a treatment while we were there. I waited in the ER waiting room while he received his treatment. It was an education as the room was pulsating with the bleeding and dying from the city—accidents, gun shot wounds etc. I wondered how the emergency room personnel could keep on full alert for the total time of their shift. It did not appear all of them were on full alert! Ralph was a wonderful, gentle person with a poet's soul and a rich tenor voice. He had been a special friend to my brother Glenn. His body was cremated and returned to Hesston. Memorial services were celebrated in Pasadena and Hesston.

During my tenure at Hesston College we also added our first grandchildren, Jana was born to Dan and Marla in Florida, and Julie when they were living in Lenexa, KS. We were privileged to see them both shortly after they were born. It made our hearts swell with pride.

Our youngest daughter Beth married Mark Goertz during this period of time, as well. Their family was blest with daughters Laura and Saundra and they have all contributed to the tapestry of our clan in a significant way.

At Whitestone Jerry Weaver resigned as pastor and Paul Brunner became our next pastor. He had a different style than Jerry that appealed less to the student population from the college so attendance was lower although membership continued strong. Paul was very active in the music program of the church and during the time Martha was going through the difficult times relating to the deaths in her family, Paul served as director of the church choir. Grace was very active in forming small groups within the congregation. We were active in a small group during their tenure. We moved to Harper the year before Paul and Grace left Whitestone.

As the time came for the completion of his fourth three-year term Laban decided it was time to move on. He had a good run with significant progress made in numerous areas with new career programs in place and enrollment at record highs. In spite of the progress it was time for a fresh approach. I was asked again to serve on the search committee. We had gone through the process and a candidate was selected who came for a visit to the campus. At the end of that visit the committee decided to extend an invitation to him. He was an individual about my age and someone with a background in teaching and preaching.

The next week, when I was fund raising in Pennsylvania, I received a call from a fellow administrator who said that the faculty had serious reservations about his appointment and felt they had not been heard in the selection process. This was the beginning of the process to withdraw the invitation. We soon realized we would need to select an interim president.

James Mininger, the dean, was asked to fill that slot. One of the first actions he took was to change the organizational structure by putting me full time into development. We were raising funds for an auditorium gymnasium, later named Yost Center, and he felt they needed my undivided attention to that endeavor. The business office and auxiliary services were assigned to Nelson Kilmer. I told Jim that I would take the assignment but would leave the college after the completion of the year and the fund raising effort for the Yost Center. I was a bit miffed that Jim, as interim president, made the move when he had only a one-year assignment. I knew I was not cut out to spend full time on development so the new president would need to find his own person for that assignment.

Lyle Yost had told Laban, when Laban hired me, "Howard will do you an excellent job as a finance man but I don't see him in fund raising." I was able to show Lyle how he could give $500,000 to the college without creating undue hardship to him and his estate. Lyle was right, fund raising was outside of my comfort zone, but the Lord gave me what I needed to work outside my comfort zone relatively effectively. Getting the lead gift from him was particularly gratifying.

Son Phil had major input into the brochure that we used for raising funds for the new building. The brochure featured schematic drawings of the building and its uses. It was done with blue print on white stock. It was inexpensive but very effective. Bill Mason was very helpful on the design and "pitch" for the piece. Phil did all of the drawings.

The next person who was chosen was Kirk Alliman who had spent most of his career working for Church World Service. Martha and I met him and his wife Jean at the Wichita airport when they arrived and had lunch with them. We became good friends over time but it was obvious to me early on that I would not have been a fit on his team. I was close to his father's age and I think it was a relief to both of us he did not have to make the decision if I should stay or go—the decision had already been made.

It is always important to leave before you're asked to—it's substantially less painful. I found something out about myself. I usually blame myself if things I'm responsible for don't turn out well. I don't need someone else to verify it or blame me for what I already feel responsible for. Don't pile it on!

Dewey Hostetler had invited me to serve on the board of DewEze Manufacturing Company while I was still employed at the college so when he found out I would be leaving the college he invited me to Harper to run the company. We didn't want to leave Hesston so he and I looked at a location in Moundridge to purchase a company there and I could oversee both operations from there. We decided against the acquisition. On Thanksgiving Day of 1980 we talked to our children about the possibility of our move to Harper. They gave unanimous approval if it was something we wanted to do. The die was cast.

I needed to complete the funding for the new building on the college campus before I left. There was a lot of support for the project and we were able to get the necessary commitments during the 1980-81 school year.

We located a building site for our home in rural Harper, moved a camper trailer to the building site, and started the construction in February of 1981. We spent a month at DewEze and then returned to Hesston for a month to complete my work assignment at the college. This was my second transition where I was working at my second job before completing my first one. By May the funds had been raised and I started working full time at DewEze.

I had some questions when leaving Hesston College. Do I have what it takes to get back into the business world and where should that be? Do I still have marketable skills at age fifty-five? Why does the church institution *feel* so much like a secular institution in the way they conduct business?

Musings about my work years at Hesston College

The years at Hesston, much of them out of my comfort zone, were excellent years. I would not have been able to move directly to DewEze Manufacturing from Hesston Corporation—the change would have been too dramatic. By cushioning the change by a hiatus of years at the college made the transition possible.

I enjoyed the work environment at the college very much. Laban was a blithe spirit with so many ideas needing to be implemented. Laban actually made me believe I could do development work! The opportunity to work with the development personnel from other educational institutions resulted in life-long friendships. Working with creative supervisors both at Hesston College and Hesston Corporation were wonderful gifts to me. My strength was in implementation, not in creation.

I needed to make contacts on the basis of those who had the *capacity* to help. Making contacts on the basis of *capacity* bypassed a lot of persons I normally would see. I never made friends on that basis. At the same time I had the opportunity to meet many individuals who had financial capacity who were most generous with their money and time. It was an advantage for me to have had a background in business. I spoke their language. It was also a time of unrest for the youth in the country and there were numbers of individuals who bared their souls concerning problems being experienced with their children. We were not untouched by those problems ourselves.

I suppose it would be fair to say I was a little hurt by the decision of the interim president to put me full time in development. However, life only has a forward gear—as friend Allen Schrag says "Bad things happen in reverse." It was the nudge I needed to add a new chapter to my life.

The Harper Years (1981-1996)

Martha had spent all of her life in Hesston and I all but the first fourteen years. She was the only one of her siblings that had remained in Kansas but now that both of her parents were deceased she had an opportunity to try out a new community. Having the prospect to plan and build a new house was a joyous experience for her. She thoroughly enjoyed planning, designing and building. With a travel trailer on site it was very easy to work with the builder, Paul Shue, and his sons Brad and Terry. It kept her occupied while I was spending some time sweating with the mounting deficits over at DewEze. It was a dilemma I didn't share with her for fear it would spoil her joy. I was exercising my normal frugality which she interpreted as just that—nothing more.

(With good friend Tom Sawin who helped us move to Harper)

When I consented to move to Harper I insisted on being not only named general manager but president of the company. Dewey had been counseled by an uncle he should take some other role than general manager because his talents could be best utilized in product development rather than in management. He accepted the evaluation and hired a succession of general managers that in a short time would come up lacking and then be terminated. If I would be terminated I wanted it to be by board action rather than as a clash with Dewey. Dewey did not have any problem consenting because he wanted me to come very badly. The wisdom of becoming president, from my perspective, was upheld a few years later. It should also be noted I was hired to replace the general manager who stayed on as sales manager. He was an ambitious young man and adapted to the demotion but kept his options open and left within a couple years.

We had purchased into DewEze but rather than putting additional funds into the company I had purchased the stock from Dewey and his brother-in-law Arnold Wedel. I should have bought the stock from the company. Although the amount I invested was not huge we certainly could have used the extra funds as the company experienced problems from the downturn in the agricultural

(Our home in the country in Harper)

economy. Additionally the prime rate for borrowing was over twenty percent—we were paying the bank twenty-four percent interest and had maxed out on our borrowing by the late summer of 1981. Our line of credit was with a bank in the neighboring town of Anthony but I approached the bank in Harper about securing a line of credit with them. The president of the bank was our neighbor and the person from whom we had purchased our three-acre tract of land for our home. The vice-president of the bank met with me and gave me the coldest reception I ever received from a banker. A couple years later, he heard via the grapevine, we were debt free, so came by to see if they could be of any service to us. I was much more civil than he had been to me—I didn't even remind him of the time when he was completely uninterested in talking to me!

The couple years before we moved DewEze had done quite well with their new bale handling equipment, particularly the truck-mounted unit. Sales were very seasonal, however, with good sales from August through January and then minimum sales during the spring and summer months. In the fall of 1979 they had been particularly inundated with sales and decided rather than adding to their current facilities to buy a vacant facility across town, a distance of almost one and a half miles. Most of the fabrication took place at the new plant and assembly and shipping over on the east side of town at the original site. The office with sales and engineering were also on the east side. This was a most cumbersome arrangement. The foreman at the west plant would say, "When the parts leave here they are made correctly, in the right quantity and on time." The foreman at the east plant would say, "When the parts arrive at the east plant they are wrong, the quantity is short and they are late." The couple restaurants along the way also beckoned the thirsty or hungry deliverer of the parts. It took at least a half hour to make a visit to the plant on the west side. I always resented the half hour of time when it would have been five or ten minutes if it was located on site.

It was obvious what needed to be done. I worked with the general foreman at the home plant on a layout that would include all of the functions of both plants. There were some detractors but we went ahead with the plans. We moved everything to the home plant and sold the west building at auction along with some excess equipment. In a short time we returned to profitability. I have been *very* wary of offsite plants or warehouses ever since.

In our fiscal year ending October 31, 1982 we lost almost a fourth of the net worth of the company. The following year we broke even and going forward never had a loss year during my tenure. Since I left in 1996 they have been profitable every year, as well. Even though I had served on the board I was relatively unaware of some of the problems facing this small company. It was not a very prudent move for us. If I had been more cautious we probably would not have risked the move and then would have missed out on all the benefits of future years. I am not sure if there is a lesson to be learned or not. Maybe it is at least partly to trust your heart, not just your head.

(Howard and Dewey with Bankers in plant)

The stress of losing money and dealing with the challenges took its toll. Just before Christmas in 1982 I was hospitalized with a bleeding ulcer. I almost never had suffered from headaches but had regular bouts of acid indigestion and pain in the abdomen. After hospitalizing me Dr. Bellar recommended taking Zantac, at the time a prescription drug, a regimen which made stomach aches largely disappear. I have taken some kind of an antacid ever since.

We withdrew our membership from Whitestone the Sunday before we left and were accepted into membership at the Pleasant Valley Mennonite Church the second Sunday we were there with Dewey and Bernie standing beside us. We were immediately invited to join a small group of about eight persons. Some of them were older than us and some younger than our own children. We enjoyed the group very much—they were eager students and didn't have a lot of pressing agenda which tends to sap the energy of the group. Shortly after arriving Martha was asked to form and direct a church choir which she did for several years. The second year we were there I was asked if I would serve as congregational chair. I called my good friend and former pastor Paul Brunner who had taken a pastorate in Ohio about taking that assignment. He opined I should probably wait a year or two until I had a better feel for the congregation. In the course of the phone conversation I asked, "Why is it OK for you to take a pastorate where you are the 'main man' while I ought to wait to accept church chair?" He didn't give me a good answer so I accepted the call.

Another major change for Martha, after the house was completed, was the phone seldom rang. I was busy at the business and my phone was active enough. She enjoyed the solitude for the most part but it came as somewhat of a revelation to her that no one "knew her history." She developed deep friendships over time but there was a period of loneliness living in the country for the first time of her life. I drove the three miles home for lunch when I was in town or didn't have a lunch meeting. We had a beautiful view from our bay window where we placed our small tea cart. We had a 250-degree vista of the east to south to west ever changing sky. After lunch I would fall off my chair onto the carpeted floor and immediately go to sleep for five to ten minutes. It was a wonderful ritual.

(Prototype slope mower at our place)

We weren't too many years into our time at DewEze before Dewey and I started experiencing some tension. We were vastly different. One of our distributors called us "the odd couple." Dewey and his brother Delmar had primary responsibility for developing products. It was particularly important for Dewey to have a new product to show at the Western Kansas 3I show each spring. Customers would come by the booth to find out what new product Dewey had come up with now. Dewey and Delmar were very creative and had good eyes for design. My questions usually were around two things: could we sell them and could they be manufactured economically? Even though the cosmetic designs were good but with short-run production and limited tooling, could they be produced cost-effectively? For both of these questions there can be honest differences of opinion. Fortunately we were profitable enough by this time to have some latitude on making those decisions.

A slope mower had been produced in Harper, not by DewEze, a number of years before I arrived on the scene. The company had long since gone bankrupt but there was a local gentleman, Ray Forpahl, who said their concept was all wrong and he would like to have the opportunity to build a prototype of his concept. He briefly described it to Dewey and me. We agreed to pay him for time and material to develop the unit in his own shop. If we decided it could be manufactured and if patents issued we would pay him a royalty. He readily agreed to the proposal. He developed a relatively crude prototype that had some unusual and intriguing concepts. We went ahead with patent applications on the new concepts and took the prototype into our engineering shop to develop a production unit. I got caught in the triangle between the shop, myself and Dewey/Delmar. The unit was not ready for production in its current form from my perspective. Substantial changes were made to the unit before it was released to production but there were hard feelings and tensions among all the parties.

We muddled through this conflict and eventually got a producible unit that was satisfactory to most all of the parties involved. Some significant patents were issued and we paid Ray Forpahl for the seventeen-year life of the patents that ensued. He was very appreciative. I was glad for the part DewEze had played in being good corporate citizens in our dealings with him. He was a hydraulic systems expert and continued to give input in subsequent years. Unfortunately Ray took his life some time after we left Harper. He had become severely depressed over his health condition and was unable to face it.

Having grown up with Hesston Manufacturing when they were small and later working with small companies that we acquired I knew something about how they functioned. DewEze had some distinct strengths. We had an excellent accountant, a competent sales force and a good plant with long term employees. We never had a layoff in all of the years that I was there. DewEze was known as a good place to work. The workers with farm background were the backbone of the work force. They not only had an appreciation for the equipment but had a good work ethic. A weakness was that many of the employees didn't have the full appreciation for what a good piece of equipment should look like when it leaves the shop floor. Many of them, in their own lives, got along with marginal equipment and were used to fixing things on their own if they didn't function. Buying new equipment was not something they did.

During a serious snow storm when the roads were closed I was looking for a day by the fire with a good book. I liked to "go with the flow" on a day like that. I suddenly was aware of the sound of a tractor and saw that Dewey had come to "rescue" me. He had come from the west a half mile through the field to allow me to get to work. I followed his snow plow to work and repeated the procedure in the evening. Snow was a challenge to him that needed to be overcome and not something you let determine your agenda. It also was an opportunity to check out the effectiveness of the DewEze pull-dozer, one of our products. Dewey was a skilled pilot who loved getting into the air for a bit of relaxation. One time, when Martha was out in the front yard, he came up behind her from the west about twenty-five or thirty feet above the ground and scared the whatever out of her. It was not an unusual prank for him but Martha failed to see the humor. He enjoyed those types of pranks.

Because both Dewey and Delmar farmed it was not always possible for them to be on the job when needed. Dewey and I decided to hire an engineer to head up our engineering effort and add more structure and formality to the process. David Landsdowne, a certified engineer was hired and served us effectively for several years. This was not an easy fit. Although David was very competent, relating to Dewey and Delmar was not easy, since Dewey was a major owner of the company. David conducted himself as a Christian gentleman but decided to seek employment elsewhere and moved to Hutchinson. We then brought Alan Bergkamp, a self-taught engineer, into the company. Dewey was a fan of Alan because he, like Dewey, was extremely creative at solving engineering problems. Over time Dewey was less enthusiastic about Alan but they maintained a decent relationship during Alan's tenure.

I discovered during this time that I enjoyed the engineering effort of our business. Dewey had fresh ideas that he shared and it was fun brainstorming with him. I don't think my contribution was extremely significant but I enjoyed the ride and learned from the process.

We tried on several occasions to secure marketing outlets through larger, better-established companies. One early attempt was to sell our Super-Slicer paired with our bale bus to the Hesston Corporation. I'm not sure who all came from DewEze for the demonstration but I know Dewey and I were there. It was a dismal failure. The bales they had for us to process were more than the Super-Slicer could handle and we had to withdraw from the field. It was a rather dismal performance in front of my former comrades.

On a couple occasions we had negotiations with Toro about either branding our small slope mower with the Toro name or possibly selling the product line to them. One such time Dewey and I were visiting with John Szafranski, senior vice-president for commercial products for Toro, about selling them our unit. At the time our power source was an air-cooled Lister-Petter engine. They were not interested in that power package because they believed the wave of the future was diesel, water-cooled power plants. During the discussion John asked whether we had thought of a tricycle arrangement for our current two-wheel version. That noon at lunch I drew the concept for the three wheel version with input from

Dewey. We dated and notarized the document and put it in the files at Harper. This documentation was to establish the date of the concept for later possible patent applications. Eventually this concept was developed by Heber Ramer and some strong patents were issued for what became the ATM-144, a twelve-foot mower for serious slope mowing. Since

(Our family at John and Chris Wedding – 1989)

Dewey had a number of patents to his name, my name was put on the patent application—the only one to ever bear my name.

During the time we lived in Harper our other seven grandchildren were born. Jana and Julie were born before we moved but were too young to remember when we lived in Hesston. All of our grandchildren only knew about our home in Harper. They enjoyed visiting Grandpa and Grandma in the country and we loved having them visit. The second year we were living in Harper I received a call from Tim Penner, an MCC worker in Bolivia, asking for our blessing to marry our daughter Faith. Faith was also a volunteer in Bolivia. I asked him "Do we have a choice?" Faith had been gone from home a number of years and was making her own way. We appreciated being asked and we extended our full blessing. I met Tim for the first time the week before their marriage. They were married at our church in Harper between Christmas and New Year in 1983.

In 1989 John and Christine Petrocci were married at the Hoffnungsau Mennonite Church in rural Buhler. All of our children were now happily married. We felt blest.

The financial ownership of DewEze was a little out of the ordinary. It was a small company with over thirty stockholders. The Lehman family of Dewey's wife, Bernie, represented the largest block of shareholders. Prior to my arrival on the scene when Dewey had needed some additional capital he had invited his in-laws to buy in. Most of them had relatively token amounts except for Arnold Wedel who owned a noteworthy amount of stock and served on the board of directors. We needed all of the cash generated by the business to expand so did not feel it was prudent to pay dividends. Even though the large group of minority stockholders was not complaining about their investment there was no easy way for them to cash out. This is part of the background for the decision in about 1990 to look for a suitable buyer for the company.

We had changed our primary bank for financing our operations to the Union National Bank of Wichita in the mid-1980s. When Martha and I had to sign a personal guarantee of a million dollars it caught Martha's attention more than mine. How could we deliver if called upon? Dewey and Bernie also had to sign a similar guarantee. We enjoyed a very good relationship with the Union National Bank until we sold the company. Also key during this time was the auditing firm of Allen, Gibbs and Houlik, also from Wichita, that handled our audit as well as serving as business consultants. Paul Allen provided very valuable input during the late 1980s and early 1990s.

In the spring of 1990 we went to visit our brother-in-law John W. Snyder and his wife Lois in Ontario. Lois was Martha's sister and was dying from a malignant brain tumor. They were special friends to us. We made a number of spontaneous trips with them on various occasions that were very memorable. To see Lois not able to communicate was difficult for both Martha and me. A poignant moment happened when Martha was holding Lois's hand singing "Jesu, Priceless Treasure" and Lois started to move her hand to the beat and tears ran down her cheeks from under her closed eyes.

We returned in August for her memorial service. Lois was a gifted musician and the singing group she had been a part of provided the music. It was a fitting memorial in song. She died just short of her sixty-fifth birthday.

In early December of 1991 John married Iva Taves, who was a medical doctor. She and her first husband were special friends to John and Lois before his death. They have had a good life together.

(Our fortieth wedding anniversary)

When we first moved to Harper, Elmer Wyse was the pastor. His wife was a distant cousin of mine, originally from Oregon. He was not a dynamic speaker but an absolutely trustworthy and committed Christian. Although he was not dynamic his sermons were always well thought out and had significant content. I think many in the congregation could not see past his lack of eloquence to the meat of his message. He resigned three years after we came. Weldon Martens became pastor and remained so for the following eleven years we were there. This was Weldon's first pastorate. He was a dynamic speaker and was very much appreciated in the community and was often called on for weddings and funerals. During his tenure he was the community minister for many of the unchurched. I was chair of the church when he first began and I sensed that he was a little uneasy with me. I was a father figure and that could have been part of the uneasiness of our beginning relationship. Even though the reason for the unease is strictly conjecture on my part we became good friends and have continued a warm relationship. Pleasant Valley Mennonite Church became much more open to the larger community during his tenure and a number of persons became members of the church.

Weldon was asked by the Harper Grade school if he could coach the seventh grade girls' team in basketball. He, in turn, asked the elders for permission. He had been a good player and enjoyed the game so we gave him permission. I think the team only won one game his first year of coaching. When he approached us the second year we asked him "What was your record last year?" The response was only a faint smile. We gave him permission to coach again.

(Our group with Albert and Lois in the Chaco of Argentina)

In 1988 we traveled with Ron and Esther Graber, Martha's sister, to South America. Tim and Faith were in Bolivia with MCC and Martha's brother Albert and Lois Buckwalter were in the Chaco of Argentina working among the Indians. We stopped in Bolivia first and then Faith, Tim and little Jessica traveled with us to Paraguay, northern Argentina to visit Albert and Lois, then to Iguaçu falls in Brazil. At this juncture Ron and Esther flew to Buenos Aires and the rest of us flew to Sao Paulo and then back to Bolivia. Ron had told me that he would take the medication along in the event we got "tourismo" but he left for BA with his medication and I got the "tourismo" in Sao Paulo. It had rained heavily when we were in Asunción, Paraguay and the streets were running full with what looked like raw sewage to me. The taxi we took to the airport did not have windows that could be closed and at an intersection my face was completely doused with the aforementioned sewage. Tim and Faith were with us and knew about such maladies so that was very helpful. I was more like steerage than a live passenger going back to Santa Cruz but I survived. It was a wonderful trip for the most part and we enjoyed visiting family and their work.

When Tim and Faith completed their assignment in Bolivia they returned to the U. S. and Tim took a position with MCC as interim regional director for Central and South America. During this time he wrote expressing an interest in working for a "for profit" business, preferably manufacturing. He asked if I knew of any company like DewEze that would be a good fit for him. I told him I didn't know of any other company like DewEze but I did know DewEze if he was interested in working for us. I visited with Dewey about this because Tim was family and Dewey heartily approved. We offered Tim the position of Administration Manager and he came to work. Tim and Faith bought the very nice two-story house in Harper that David Lansdowne had for sale when he left DewEze. Tim sold himself immediately as more than the boss's son-in-law and became a valuable member of the team. It also was the first time that we lived in the same community as any of our grandchildren!

In an attempt to get a better understanding of the dissonance that had developed between Dewey and myself we decided to get some counseling. We asked an experienced mediator with whom we both felt comfortable, to help us. We met in Wichita with Nelson Galle for the session. He first talked to Dewey for an hour and then talked to me for an hour. During that time we both explained our discomfort in the relationship. After the two sessions we all met together. Nelson said "Dewey, this is what I heard you say about your problems with Howard and you can't interrupt while I tell him." He reversed the process for me. We both knew we had to work together for the good of the company but it was a struggle for both of us. The session was helpful in clearing the air and helped ameliorate the problem but did not solve it. It opened communication somewhat.

Although not directly related to this dissonance, Dewey and Bernie and the other major stockholders were ready to sell the company at this point. We did some inquiry about the best way to go about the process and ended up registering with a broker to sell. The first company that approached us was the Alamo group from Seguin, TX. They were the largest supplier of bat wing mowers in the US and were particularly interested in our large slope mower. They made a tentative offer which was attractive and I made a visit to Seguin to their plant to look more closely if it would be a fit for us. It became obvious the company ethos was not something compatible with us. The feeling I got if summarized in one word was "distrust." Fortunately, we were spared the decision because they withdrew their offer. I believe they withdrew their offer because they did not see the DewEze large mower (then a two-wheeled model) as a viable product for the highway market. They really weren't interested in the rest of the products we produced and I think would have spun them off if they had purchased us.

(Celebrating the sale to Owosso – Howard, Bernie, Dewey and Martha)

The second suitor to come calling was the Owosso Corporation out of Philadelphia. They were a mini-conglomerate with a number of operating units in diverse product fields. They had decided to get into the agricultural market and purchase some small entities in niche markets. George Lemon Jr., or Geordie, as they called him, handled the bulk of the negotiations from their side. He was the son of one of the founders and was a bright young guy who wanted to do his first acquisition right. I immediately liked him as well as the company he represented. We were able to come to an amicable agreement and they completed the purchase in 1991. Part of their method of purchase included letting persons whom they were purchasing from buy ten percent of the new company. They offered five percent to Dewey and five percent to me. This again demonstrated the difference between a true entrepreneur and a manager type. Dewey was not at all interested in buying into the new company he would have minimum input into. Since Dewey turned his five percent stake down I was offered ten percent which I took immediately. I did not have to give any guarantees and was on an equal footing as the other Owosso individuals who bought in. There was a buyout plan in place in the event I decided I wanted out and I was well acquainted with what I bought. Dewey, the entrepreneur, didn't understand why I bought back in when I had just sold my shares. They had invited me to stay on as president and both of us were given five year "non-compete" bonuses so, since I wasn't ready to retire, it seemed like an excellent opportunity. The tension that had built up between Dewey and me, although largely under the surface, had finally been relieved. Dewey stayed on as a consulting engineer for a year or so and then left to pursue other interests.

Owosso's operating policy was to buy small to medium sized companies that were profitable and let them operate with a minimum of corporate interference. This was the way they operated. Monthly I would send a written report along with financial statements to Tom French, their president. I knew what they wanted and was able to deliver with a minimum of effort. The five years I worked for Owosso were the five most stress-free years of my working life. They called me on a regular basis and visited from time to time. Yearly the company presidents would get together at some resort for a minimum of work and a maximum amount of playing golf and eating fine food. The agenda for the week was on two typewritten pages. I was serving on the Mennonite Board of Missions at the time we had our annual meeting at Tarpon Springs, FL. I went directly to Elkhart, IN from Tarpon Springs. The agenda for our board of missions meeting was at least two inches thick! Either the Owosso agenda was underkill or the Mission Board meeting was overkill. It might have been symbolic of their respective importance! In later years, after I left, Owosso was profoundly changed with new management.

Tim and Faith lived in a part of town that had a lot of children and they loved to congregate at their place. After school and during the summer there were a number of children who seemed to go around largely unsupervised. Tim and Faith approached us about trading houses. Tim liked the rural setting with the possibility of some livestock and garden and Faith wanted less traffic from the neighborhood children. Martha liked the old large house in town and immediately had some designs for improving it. We agreed to have both of our houses appraised to set the selling price. Our house in the country appraised somewhat higher than the one in town. There was some discussion about negotiating for a smaller differential but we ended up trading for the difference in the appraised values.

(Our last house in Harper)

Owosso owned a company called Kuker-Parker with plants in Omaha, NE and Jefferson, IA. They decided to consolidate the plants in Jefferson, IA. They determined to set up the consolidated entity as a subsidiary of DewEze. They wanted to reward certain persons who had the most invested in DewEze. I was not one of the persons they were particularly interested in rewarding but being one of the owners of DewEze I got a free ride! This also would give me the oversight of the Parker plant. Tim had worked at DewEze for two years and was getting a little restless in his current position. Owosso was aware that he was a budding talent and picked him for the Parker assignment. He first went to the plant in Omaha and closed it down and then moved the balance of the operations to Jefferson.

A humorous event happened in Boston when I was attending a trade show with some of our products. Geordie Lemon had come up from Philadelphia and had lunch with me in downtown Boston. On the way back to the show Geordie was telling me about all of the places along the way as if he was very familiar with the area. I inquired as to why he knew the area so well. He replied "I went to college here." "Oh, I said, where?" He replied "Harvard." I had known that information from another source but I said "Most people brag about graduating from Harvard, why are you apologetic about it?" "The people I want to impress are more impressed if you haven't graduated from Harvard than if you have," was his reply.

I had been asked to serve on the board of Great Bend Manufacturing Company by their board in about 1990, I believe. The president of the company was Max Bennett whom I had known from Hesston Manufacturing days. While I served on the board I was invited to purchase some of their stock from an investor who wanted to cash out. About a year after I purchased the stock the Owosso Company purchased them. I was given half of my compensation for the stock in cash and the other half in a note from Owosso. I felt a *little* guilty that I received five times the amount I had paid for the stock a year after I purchased it. Some years later, when Owosso was in financial trouble, I was asked by Owosso to settle the remaining balance due on the note for about forty percent of its face value. We had met in Wichita with the group that held the notes and I was of the opinion that it was as good as we were going to do. This seemed to turn the tide and everyone bought off on the offer. George Lemon, Jr. had made the pitch and being the straight shooter he was I felt it would be as good an offer as we could get. Forcing them into bankruptcy would only give more to the lawyers, not us. I received a very nice letter from Geordie after the meeting thanking me for being an advocate for him. A motto I tried to live by—always look at what you have received, not what you left on the table.

(Our last reunion with brothers in 1991 –John, Grace, Lois, Lloyd, Pearl, Martha, Howard, Gladys, James)

Some *very* painful and distressing events took place in the spring of 1993. We were in the midst of trading houses with Tim and Faith. Martha and I had gone to Wichita and returned to the house in town where Tim and Faith were still living. We were outside looking at the shingling of the new attached garage when Faith came out and told us that she had just received word that my youngest brother John had died. He was an avid runner and had just come into his back yard in Denver and dropped over from a heart attack. I was stunned. He was still very active as the administrator of the Spaulding Rehabilitation Hospital in Denver. How could this be? We, of course, went to the funeral in Denver for a celebration of his life. Everyone loved John and the outpouring of love and admiration was dramatic. My brother James and brother-in-law Lloyd were also there. There were recordings of some of the groups John sang with including the male quartet that was front and center in his life. He was only sixty.

Tim and Faith were living with us while we completed the changes we were making to the house in town. We had just returned from the house in town to our house in the country when Tim met us at the head of the stairs and told me my brother James had died. This was ten days after John had died. James was a more likely candidate for death than John because he was experiencing kidney failure and was on dialysis. He was still active as the administrator of a retirement community in Orrville, OH and he also had dropped over while taking a walk in the evening with his wife, Gladys. They had not lived in Orrville for many years so did not have the host of connections there that John did in Denver. Additionally it was Easter and a number of persons were gone. The celebration of his life was quieter but they had a recording of him singing "I am the Bread of Life" which he had sung at the last communion service at their church. Brother-in-law Lloyd Rodgers was at the funeral. James was only sixty-two.

One month later on Mother's Day our family all got together, as is the custom, for dinner at Chris and John's place. I had the flu and stayed home. While at home I received word Lloyd had passed away. Lloyd was sixty-nine when he died. He had been receiving chemo treatment for a malignancy. They were treating it aggressively but during this time he contracted pneumonia and with the weakened resistance succumbed to the disease. It was devastating. Suddenly in just over one month I was the only male survivor among my siblings. I felt guilty to be alive!

Suddenly things that had seemed very important to me faded into irrelevance. I was devastated. We hadn't been in contact that often with each other. The family circle letter came by almost every month but we were all living our separate lives apart from each other. The sense of loss I felt was multiplied many times over for my sister and my sisters-in-law and I deeply empathized with them. Martha too was traumatized by the events. I probably buried myself in my work to alleviate the pain but I soon resigned from the Mennonite Board of Missions. Responsibilities outside my primary work needed to be cut back. I didn't fear it would soon be me but it didn't make sense that all of them should be taken when each of them was in a productive period of their lives. Eventually I was at peace but the scars are still there.

In 1994, after their deaths, we had a family reunion north of Edmonton, Alberta. I had been asked to give a tribute to my brothers when we met at the Salem Mennonite Church in Tofield. It was also the burial site of my brother Kenneth, whom I never knew. I wrote it out but was unable to deliver it because of the pain and emotion I was still experiencing. Martha read the tribute for me.

We finished our remodeling of the town house in 1993 and completed our move. The addition to the house included a two car attached garage and a hot tub and laundry room on the main floor. We opened up the back stairway that had been used when there was a second floor apartment. This stairway opened into the laundry and spa room. Phil helped with the design of fitting the garage onto the old house built in 1906. It was a good fit. During the remodeling process I got a nasal infection, I assume from the dust of prior years. I did not completely get rid of the infection until we moved to our new home in Hesston several years later. Meanwhile, shortly after trading houses with Tim and Faith, they moved to Ames, Iowa to manage the plant at Jefferson. They rented their house to a DewEze employee while they were gone for two years.

Later that year DewEze was awarded "the company of the year" award by the Owosso group. This came as a complete surprise. This award was always announced at the annual president's meeting. DewEze had an excellent year in 1993 but I don't know how they decided we were to receive the award. The first prize was a trip to anywhere in the world with your spouse. The second prize was $500. We chose to go to Australia and New Zealand. This decision was based on the most far off place in the world that spoke the English language.

We had a wonderful time with a tour group of twenty-eight persons from all over the United States. Although we were all on the same flight to Auckland, NZ we didn't know they were part of our group until we arrived at our hotel. We spent ten days in NZ traveling by bus primarily and then eleven days in Australia. We particularly enjoyed NZ. A highlight of the trip was a helicopter ride from Queensland to Mitre Peak. It is the highest mountain in the world directly adjacent to the ocean. We were scheduled to go by boat but because of high water and wind they canceled that part of the trip. A doctor from Iowa was incensed at the cancellation and decided to take a helicopter if he could find someone with whom to share the cost of $1000. We volunteered so the doctor and his wife with Martha and I and a New Zealand *hot dog* pilot made the memorable trip. We saw spectacular falls up close and personal that we never could have seen by boat. My rationalization for spending $500 was that we had a free trip and this seemed like too good a chance to miss. My mother would not have approved! Martha barely did but she agreed afterwards that it was worth the price of admission. We stayed in touch with one of the couples for a little while but have since lost track of them.

A special time was in Cairns, Australia. We had gone out to the Coral Reefs for the day and in the evening when we came back we had a free evening. Martha and I walked toward town from our hotel and stopped at a small café for dinner. As we were eating a recording was played of Enya, the Welsh folk singer, singing, "My life goes on in endless song." The date was one year after the death of my brother John and it was a song that was sung at his funeral. It was a touching moment for both of us.

One morning I called the Owosso office in Philadelphia and started the conversation with their receptionist with my normal "Ahhhhh" and she replied, "Why, good morning, Howard." She did not need caller ID to identify me! It was hilarious for me and a joke that my friends enjoyed, as well.

The Owosso Company decided to go public so there would be a market for their stock and an opportunity for some of the original owners to cash out. I had put in my two cents worth about the dangers of public ownership and the pressures for performance. They assured me it would be different for them. Famous last words! For that reason, and possibly others, the company began to change. The company was a conglomerate of well-run companies producing good products and good profits. Some of the original owners were wanting out and some of them the Owosso management wanted out. They started bringing in "professional managers" who had impeccable credentials but had never run a company. Most of the old managers just put their hot hand on the business they were running and knew intuitively if it was going well or not. They also knew how to fix it without elaborate systems. A new president was hired to replace Tom French. The new one needed "two-inch-thick reports." Some years after

I left the company was virtually bankrupt and only avoided bankruptcy by selling to another company. I still own a small number of shares of the subsequent company.

After I retired we gifted a lot of the stock we had acquired from Owosso. I was not able to sell or give the stock away for two years after the initial offering because of SEC regulations. By then the stock had depreciated. We eventually gave most of it away. The charity that we gave it to sold it immediately so they got their cash and somebody else took a hit as the stock continued to decline in value. In a real sense what we had left of this investment was what we had given away.

I had set a target date of retiring at age seventy and had shared it with Tom French, the Owosso president. By the spring of the year when I would be turning seventy in the fall I was beginning to feel the heat. They were looking for young ambitious managers and I wasn't one of them. Why not move the date up a little. They gave Tim the opportunity of either staying with Parker in Jefferson, IA or moving back to Harper to manage DewEze. Both Tim and Faith wanted to be closer to family with their children as well as wanting to be closer to their church. They opted for the DewEze job and I resigned effective April 1, 1996.

On the Saturday evening of my retirement they held a dinner party and "roast" at the senior center in Harper. It was a wonderful event. The eulogies poured in—it was like being at your own funeral without dying. Tom French was not there but sent a very flattering message. Lyle Yost was there and gave a nice tribute. A number of our other Hesston friends were present. There was a pall that I felt but couldn't share. I knew that Monday morning several key persons would get their notice of termination. Some of them said some nice things about me, as well. The decisions of the organizational change were mostly coming directly from Owosso but Tim needed to approve them. I told Tom French, the Owosso president "This might play in Philadelphia where no one knows the players but it's trouble in Harper."

There were five individuals terminated. I was not present on the Monday it happened. Tom French came out from Philadelphia and handled the terminations. With a change of management there needed to be a re-alignment of the team to better utilize the gifts of the individuals involved. They were persons who fit on my team but didn't necessarily fit on Tim's. I felt empathy for each one let go.

We had done some downsizing when we moved from the country to town. Even though the house in town had probably as many square feet as the one in the country it had a lot less cupboard space so we had set out a table and let the children and grandchildren take whatever they wanted. Not everything was taken so it had to be disposed of elsewhere. We had enough stuff that we opted to have an auction sale when we left Harper. The sale was held at the auction barn in Harper and we had an excellent crowd. There were a few other individuals who put things on the sale. The sales proceeds came to a little over $5000 which we felt was very good. We gave each of our children an amount of money, I have forgotten how much, to buy items at the sale that they could use. If they didn't use it for the sale they could do something else with it. We still have the itemized list of the sale items and what each item brought.

I had some questions on leaving the Harper years. What will I do to be productive during my next years? Will Martha be able to handle me in the house or should I rent an office? Why am I still alive when my brothers are all gone?

Musings on the Harper Years

I was present when DewEze was saved from insolvency. I don't take credit for it but it happened during my watch. Someone else could have come in and done what I did but it happened to be me. I used to tell Dewey, "Look at all of the successful operations around that have neither you nor me to guide them." I was trying to get a little perspective.

These were important years for us. The first years we had been out of the Hesston community. They also were years of an amount of stress particularly in relationships. It also marked the end of my working career. Twenty five years at Hesston Corporation, five years at Hesston College and fifteen years at DewEze. We added to our list of lifelong friends. The local paper gave some "over-the-top" compliments about my tenure at DewEze which I appreciated even though the editor engaged in some excessive hyperbole.

All of the persons on Tim's key management team were persons I had hired. This has been very gratifying to me. My business life was not over. A few years after I left Tim bought the company back from Owosso and I became part of that purchase.

The community of Harper is much more typical of small town America than Hesston. With the college and a relatively large industrial presence it is much more urban in its outlook than Harper. When asked about my political leanings I have said, "When I was in Harper I was considered to be left of center, when I came to Hesston I was considered to be right of center, so I'm probably just about right!"

I also learned a bit about how Hesston is viewed from Harper. When we came to Harper the postman, a non-Christian, told Martha "Oh I see we have someone here from the Vatican." Hesston always thought the "Vatican" was in Goshen or Elkhart. I don't know where the people in Goshen or Elkhart think the "Vatican" is but they probably think its somewhere else also. The real seat of power is somewhere you're not.

To help the self-image of the small company of DewEze I used to say, "Just because the big boys do it doesn't mean it isn't stupid." It still seems true today!

I bought into DewEze three times. On the basis of both pleasure and profit the first time it was good, the second time was excellent and the third was fantastic. The reason the last time was so special is because I didn't need to actually do much of anything. It is rather like being a grandparent. You pay a visit, give your input, and then leave the actual work to the parents. In most of the experiences in my working life I have been treated fairly. I feel like an ordinary talent who has been given extraordinary opportunities.

Beyond Maturity (1996—)

On April 1, I left the employ of DewEze and in May we moved back to Hesston. When we moved to Harper it was planned that we would return to Hesston for retirement. On June 1 we went back to Harper for our sale. It was a beautiful day and well attended. There were a lot of well wishers and the eagerness with which persons bid on our personal possessions seemed affirming.

The home we were moving to in Hesston was one of the first three-bedroom units in Lake Vista and they let Martha do a good deal of the design within the parameters outlined by the Villa. She enjoyed the opportunity to once again plan the design of a house. We have been very pleased with the results. It is a well-constructed house that is very comfortable for our needs. Martha says the kitchen is the handiest in all of her years. We have wonderful neighbors and the maintenance crew of the Villa does all of the outdoor things that I really never enjoyed doing. I have long since outgrown the need to dig in the dirt or mow the grass.

We returned to Hesston with church letter in hand and the second Sunday back were accepted into membership at Whitestone. Church membership has always been extremely important to us and keeping it current seems the responsible thing to do. When we went to Sunday school we knew all of the approximately thirty members of our Sunday school class except the teacher. Even though we had enjoyed our time in Harper a great deal, it felt like we were coming home again.

I joined the Men's group that meets every Tuesday morning at 6:30. The group has always been about ten to fourteen members and continues at that size now. We alternate between studying a book of the Bible to studying a book on the Christian life or a book that has been particularly helpful for one of the members. The group has varied over time. The average age has crept up a little over time but it continues to be a significant element of the routine for the week.

Being part of the church and its activities has continued to be front and center for both of us. We have been granted voices to sing which we have continued to use. We have attended *many* funerals and have sung at a number of them. Singing at funerals is becoming rarer as our voices become more marginal. We continue to sing with Walt and Carol Friesen at the Villa Bible study once a month. We have been participating in A Cappella for a number of years and have enjoyed the small group atmosphere and singing both the new and the old.

In September 1996, upon our return to Hesston, we took our long postponed honeymoon trip to the west coast, up into British Columbia and Alberta, stopping in Montana to visit Dan, Marla and family. It was a very special time of closeness—so much better than it would have been 48 years earlier! It definitely was worth the wait! Martha got to meet my old school teacher, Ivor Boon, in Calgary. She was very impressed!

Shortly after coming back to Hesston we started meeting with Tom and Ruby Sawin for a meal every other week. We invited John and June Zielke to join us shortly after we started. We would rotate from home to home. These were very special times of food and fellowship. It supplied food for the soul as well as food for the body. In 2000 June was diagnosed with stomach cancer. They discovered her malignancy was one very difficult to treat and decided against surgery which they deemed to be ineffective. We continued to meet during the fall and winter until the spring of 2001. She had a wonderful spirit as she succumbed to the disease. She taught us not only how to live but how to die. We were on our way to Julie's graduation in California when we received word June had died. We were so sorry to miss her funeral.

After June's death the remaining members of the group met with John occasionally to supply support to him. In a couple years he found another mate whom he had known earlier who now lived in Missouri. They were married and he moved to Missouri to live with her. John is a dear life-long friend. We continue meeting Tom and Ruby for breakfast once a week

In the spring of 2000 we had an opportunity to attend the graduation of granddaughter Jana from Liberty University in Virginia with a B.S. in nursing. After the ceremony we traveled with Dan, Marla and family to the east coast and Washington D.C. It was a special time of connecting with the Montana family whom we were seldom privileged to see.

On Labor Day of 2000 Wayne and Margie Swartzendruber went with us to Abilene on Labor Day to visit an old mansion we heard about. We were planning on eating at Brookville Hotel but found out they were closed so came home via Salina. As we were walking out of the restaurant I was reaching in my pocket for my keys and missed seeing the end of the sidewalk and fell clumsily onto the graveled parking lot. I broke four bones on my left hand. My fingers looked like raw sausages with a bone protruding from one of the fingers. We spent the next five hours in the emergency room at the Salina Hospital. Wayne drove us home after the ordeal was over.

The next week I had a heart catheterization after having some heart arrhythmia on a stress test and they discovered some heart blockage. The week following I had bypass surgery. I felt that because my cholesterol and blood pressure were under control I would not have arterial damage. Apparently I was wrong. Dr. Idbeis performed the surgery. They did not stop my heart for the surgery. I thought the surgery would probably be a "walk in the park" since all they did was take veins from my leg and replace four of the arteries in my heart! As is the custom, when ill, I was a major pain. Even though I did not change rooms every night I seemed to be in a different room with all kinds of weird things going on. On the fifth day I returned home and everything stayed in place all night long! The road to recovery was a bit rocky with some episodes of auricular fibrillation which is less than comfortable. This improved over time as the healing progressed.

In the spring of 1998 Myron and Esther Augsburger were input persons at an event at the college. At the last minute it was discovered provisions had not been made for their lodging and Bill Zuercher asked if we could take them. We were delighted to. On Sunday afternoon we took them to dinner and a performance of the Wichita Symphony. Shortly after we returned home we received a call from Tim that Faith had a near head-on collision with another car while returning from Wichita. The car had been totaled but Faith was the only one with significant injury. She had sustained facial lacerations and a cut which came very close to an artery. Myron led in a special prayer for her safety. The next day we went to Harper to help with the cleanup and to visit Faith. That evening Tim had been called to meet the management of the Owosso group in Wichita. He called right after his meeting to ask if we could stay on in Harper until he returned because he needed to talk to us.

When he returned he told us Owosso wanted to sell DewEze and were giving Tim the first opportunity to buy it. Tim had become restless working for the new Owosso and was actively looking for an opportunity to purchase his own company. This seemed like an answer to prayer if he could manage the financing of it. Seldom do you get to buy a company you know more about than the seller does. Tim and I plus four of his staff members were able to put the funds together to buy the company. With Industrial Revenue Bonds plus bank financing we were quite highly leveraged in order to make the purchase. It also included an unsecured note from Owosso—they believed in him and wanted to sell.

The organization quickly took shape and a board of directors was appointed. It was immediately renamed Harper Industries and was organized as an S Corporation. My arrangement was I would continue as a shareholder for five years and then would sell a fifth of my holdings to Tim each of the next five years. It worked out precisely as planned and I am no longer a stockholder in the company. I have continued to serve on the board and meet with Tim and his staff each month when they review their monthly operating statement. It has been a most rewarding experience. I receive the pleasure of involvement with only a minimum of the pain experienced when you operate a company. Today there are only three stockholders as two of the management persons have sold their stock back to the company. A decision made when starting the company was to give ten percent of the earnings to charity. Since the profits in an S corporation flow to the stockholders each individual determines the charity their percentage will go to. The company writes the checks to the charity so the stockholders are bound to contribute their share. It has been a source of joy for all of us involved.

On January 1, 1999 I decided to begin a newspaper for our family called *Hershberger Happenings*. The family was scattered and the grandchildren were beginning to leave their parental homes and I was concerned we would be losing track of each other. It was particularly critical for me that we keep the out-of-state families connected to those of us living in Kansas. This paper has been mostly a joy except for the pain of publication. As time has progressed most of the input has come from the children which has been very helpful. I haven't had to make as much stuff up! Over time the circulation has increased as additional persons have asked to be on the mailing list. Current circulation is twenty-five, about a maximum for my inkjet printer. Each full-color edition is three sheets printed on both sides and always contains a little foolishness as well as news. I need an outlet for my abnormal strangeness, I assume. As one of my children says "Why Howeird!"

Technology has always intrigued me. I got my first laptop computer before we left Harper and had it on my desk at work. It was a good opportunity to learn since I had technical help immediately available at the office. When I left, however, I was not very computer literate so immediately took class work in Wichita at a computer store. These were mostly one-day or two-day courses on PC applications. They were quite helpful but additionally I had more time to spend on the computer to have hands-on experience. As is the nature of technology—in spite of all I have learned there is more I don't know than when I first began. This technology *bug* has bitten me more than once but I still go back for more. I have rationalized it has been substantially less expensive than extensive traveling but I have to recognize that it is just that—rationalization. I have gradually weaned myself from needing the latest and the greatest in technology but I still occasionally get an itch just needing to be scratched so I get another gadget. I say this mostly to my shame and not my credit.

In investing in technology I have been able to do some things that have had some value. I took all of the good music we had on LPs and tapes and converted them to CDs. Again technology moves on and CDs are becoming passé. So far most everyone can still play them on the equipment they have. I also took all of the slides and a number of the prints we have and digitalized them. Rather than scanning the slides I bought a camera that had a very short focal length and using a light table took pictures of the slides. This has been more satisfactory than using an inexpensive scanner and is much faster. Even though most of what I have left is time it still is *very* important to do tasks expeditiously! I have digitalized slides for some others as well. I have also lent my light table to others so they could digitalize their own.

Another side benefit from my use of the computer was the ability to do the accounting entries for Sweetwater Farms during their early years. I have not done that for a number of years but it was a good way to get to know about their business and submit an opinion or two. (It could also be why I'm no longer doing it!!)

Staying abreast of technology has been beneficial in at least being able to carry on a semi-literate conversation with the next generation. It is also important for them to be able to show Grandpa a thing or two that he doesn't know. This is all part of the rationalization that I have gone through to justify my habit. I have as big a computer as I need for the foreseeable future (which is not very far)! My first computer had 1 gigabyte of memory, now fourteen years later, it's 500 times that big. Martha was very appreciative that I was not a profane man when I was first working in the study after we moved to Hesston. The strongest words she heard from the office were "Oh, no" which is quite mild considering the level of frustration. She seldom hears that anymore so I may have reached a higher level of proficiency on the computer.

(I was featured in *Hesston College Today* for sole patent to my name – the 144 mower)

With my 80-20 mentality I get eighty percent of the benefit with only twenty percent of the effort so I will never get really skilled at using any of the toys I have since I want to reserve the eighty percent effort for the things that are *really* important!

I thought that when I was no longer in the work force I would be interested in following the markets and reading business literature but those aren't my interests now. I have enjoyed theological books and books on the Christian life much more than investments and cutting edge business strategies. I have also included the practice of reading the Bible through at least once every year. This probably means that I serve more as a chaplain to Harper Industries than a business consultant!

I have served on a number of fund raising activities in the past fourteen years, some of them with Martha. Even though fundraising was outside my comfort zone, organizations are always looking for free help with this effort. I helped raise funds for South Central Conference operating fund, Mennonite Central Committee regional headquarters building, Hesston College on a couple different campaigns, AMBS library campaign, Mennonite Mission Network headquarters building in Elkhart, Schowalter Villa and the Whitestone building addition. One of the other criteria for volunteer fund raisers is to have the capacity to help financially. One time, when we had been asked for a million dollar gift, which we certainly didn't have the capacity to give Martha said, "Do they think we're rich?" I replied, "Isn't it nice for people to think you're rich without needing to be bothered with the money?"

(Our home at Schowalter Villa – 1996)

I also served for a couple different terms on the Schowalter Foundation board which gives money away. There were always more requests than the funds we had available to give. When I left I told them, "There is never enough money to meet all of the needs so feel good about what you *can* give and not what you *can't* give." This is how we have tried to conduct our giving. We feel extremely blest that we have been able to give what we can and take satisfaction in it.

I served South Central Mennonite Conference for two years as moderator elect and two years as moderator. This was another stretch for me. Fortunately we had both a very capable conference minister, Dick Headings, but also a very capable administrator in Bill Zuercher. This at least helped ameliorate my ineptitude. I gained a new appreciation for the work of the church and the many dedicated persons in positions of responsibility. Part of these years was when I was still at Harper. The custom had been that one term would be served by an ordained person and the next one by a lay person. That practice has since been discontinued.

In the spring of 2004 Martha's oldest brother Albert died after an extended bout with cancer. He was able to have all of his family with him at his passing. At the memorial service a CD of an excellent quartet he had been a part of during his Goshen College years provided the pre-service music. He used his passion for language to translate the Bible into several different Indian languages in the Chaco of Argentina. With his passing Martha is left with only one sibling, Esther Rose Graber.

We had a major effort at Whitestone when we connected the educational building to the main sanctuary building. I chaired the committee that had the primary responsibility. We visited a number of different churches as well as spending a good deal of time with the architects. We had an excellent committee with diverse gifts and the final results were excellent. A major disappointment of the plan was that the bids for the work came in a full twenty-five percent above the architects' estimate. The two buildings we were joining were never intended to be joined. They were at different elevations and different orientations. The architect made his estimate on the primary basis of the square footage while the contractors were looking at the complexity of marrying the two structures. We went ahead with the plans and as of the beginning of 2011 the building is fully paid for. Our people have been very generous. Martha and I ended up putting more into the building than we had planned but we are completely at peace about it.

The congregation had been polled about what they considered to be the primary lack in the current facility and what they felt were the most pressing needs. One felt need, although not a top priority, was enough sanctuary space so that we didn't need two services. This was the only expressed need not satisfied with the new addition. At this point the congregation has accepted the plan of two Sunday morning services even though less than ideal. We are thankful that our attendance is such that we need two services.

Another volunteer activity that has mostly been a joy in retirement has been taking persons from the Villa to their medical appointments. For several years I took two individuals to Newton for kidney dialysis treatments. They became good friends over time and it was sad to see them succumb to the ravages of age and disease. I do not like waiting. To overcome this proclivity I take my Kindle with me and use the waiting room of the medical office as a reading room. It works ninety percent of the time!

Good Friday morning of 2008 was a singular day. At 2:30 a.m. I woke with a very strange feeling. I went to the bathroom and felt very light headed so I felt my pulse which was exceedingly slow and irregular. I had a pulse rate between twenty-five and thirty-five. I woke Martha and said that she should probably get me to the emergency room. A wiser decision would have been to call 911. I got ready and got into the car. On the way to the emergency room, a distance of about ten miles I told Martha "If I slump over, just keep driving." Even though it was probably good advice under the circumstances I shouldn't have put her in those circumstances. When we arrived at the emergency room the doctor saw me almost immediately and then said "You need a pacemaker, but we'll have to do some lab work before we can send you on to the Kansas Heart Hospital. It is more important for the administration of this hospital to get the lab work done than to have the patient survive!" With those encouraging words I was in the emergency room for another two hours while they got the lab work completed and then forwarded me on to the Kansas Heart Hospital in Wichita. It was my first ride in an ambulance and it felt very much like I was lying on my back in a pickup truck. Martha followed with our car. We arrived at the Kansas Heart hospital at about 6:30 and they wheeled me into surgery an hour later and when I came out at 8:00 I felt like a new man. I'm healed! It was a big "Praise the Lord" moment. The pacemaker has definitely improved my quality of life. Even though I occasionally feel like my heart wants to do its auricular fibrillation thing the pacemaker doesn't let it.

Possibly because of the heavy traveling I did while at Hesston Corporation we have done virtually no traveling outside of United States and Canada during our closing years. As a couple we have always enjoyed traveling together by car. We have had a number of memorable trips by auto enjoying good food and fellowship away from our home base. We had a memorable trip to the Maritime Provinces in Canada when the whole world was a blaze of color. We experienced a unique Sunday morning service in the oldest United Church of Canada sanctuary where the poor met the wealthy and fellowshipped together. That same evening we stopped at a fund raising dinner at a Catholic church in the country and had a very good visit with a Catholic sister who was working at an abuse center in St. John. We were privileged to partake of the local cuisine. We enjoyed being in Quebec City where I got a new twist on the history of Canada from a French Canadian perspective. It reminded me again of how the same event reported from a different point of view is a quite different story.

A singular pleasure was to have five of our grandchildren attend Hesston College. All of them did their laundry at our place and they all did their own. Grandpa and Grandma were hands off. Grandma occasionally had some advice to the grandsons. How many clothes can you put in one batch and expect them to come out clean? We even served as mod parents for Ben when he was an RA his sophomore year. We were pleased to be asked to be mod *parents* when we're really *grandparents*. Although we weren't mod parents when Daniel was an RA we got to entertain his mod a couple times and it also gave us a lot of pleasure.

An extraordinary trip to California to spend quality time with our grandchildren of the Dan and Marla family stands out. We had a couple days with just the grandchildren before Dan and Marla arrived from Montana. What a special treat of connecting and affirmation with our own flesh and blood. We were privileged to meet our future grandchildren, friends Joe Young and Sarah Langenbacher, for the first time.

In the summer of 2004 we took a month-long trip to Alberta for the Brenneman reunion in Edmonton. On the way to Edmonton we stopped at High River where Mary and Ruth Guengerich had arranged for a group of about fifteen childhood school friends to meet with us for lunch. Pearl and her son Ken were also at this rendezvous. What a remarkable time! Most of them I had not seen in over sixty years but I could still pick out who they were. In some cases they looked very much like their parents, as I remembered them, only older. After the Brenneman reunion we continued up to Peace River visiting the sites of many outposts of the work of the Northwest Mennonite Conference in the frontier. We then continued over to Dawson Creek and then to Prince Rupert where we took an all-day ferry ride down the inside passage to Vancouver Island. We traveled the length of Vancouver Island to Victoria and then by ferry over to Vancouver. From there we journeyed to Banff and Jasper and on the west side of the Canadian Rockies to Idaho and Montana. We arrived in Bozeman, MT for the much-anticipated marriage of granddaughter

Julie to Joe Young. All of our children were there, except for Beth and Mark. Most of our grandchildren were there also. This was the longest time in one stretch we were away from home base in our sixty-two years of marriage.

In the spring of 2007 sister Lois H. was visiting her daughter in Topeka and had a seizure. They took her to the emergency room and after doing a number of tests determined she had a brain tumor. After additional consultation and tests they decided to operate. They were not able to remove the entire tumor and then started chemo treatments. The treatments were ineffective and after a time they moved her into the medical wing of the Villa for her last days. She passed away in November at eighty-two years of age. A special blessing for her in her latter years was the pleasure of having her daughter happily married to a fine Christian gentleman, Stephen Lowry. Steve not only courted Glenna but her mother as well—it was a winning ploy. It certainly has made the loss of her mother easier with Steve at her side. Lois was a faithful member of Whitestone and the Hershberger family. She honored Glenn in a unique way by staying closely connected to our family all of her life. We miss her.

In 2006 we journeyed to Oregon for the Hershberger family reunion. On the way we stopped at Klamath Falls, OR for a Sunday morning service at a Lutheran church. We were particularly impressed with the service and the honesty of the sharing and the individualized prayers offered. Having a natural inclination toward the liturgical it resonated with both of us. Of course the highlight on the trip was the reunion with family again. On the way home we traded cars in Salt Lake City, UT. I probably should say I traded cars since Martha saw no need to trade since our other car was working perfectly fine from her point of view. I think she was right!

In 2010 we took another trip to Alberta. The impetus for this came from our need to see our great granddaughters and parents in Great Falls, MT. It was wonderful to get acquainted with our three little *great* granddaughters. A highlight was sitting in church on Sunday evening when there were requests for songs from the congregation and four year old Annalie chose "Immortal, Invisible, God only Wise" and sang the first two verses very heartily by memory! Getting to Great Falls put us close enough to Alberta that I felt we needed to make the extra effort to go there at least one more time. We traveled through Banff and Jasper on the road to Tofield where we connected with niece Bonnie and Milo Stauffer. We attended Salem Mennonite and revisited many of the boyhood sites on

Sunday afternoon. We then journeyed to Mazeppa and relived some of those memories.

Attending church has been an important part of our life when traveling. It was not always completely enjoyable for the children when they were growing up and traveling with us particularly if we were singled out to be introduced. We worshipped with Baptist, Congregational, Presbyterian, Methodist, Mennonite, Nazarene, Lutheran and Community Churches to name a few. Once, when we were crossing a time zone we were shown into our pew in the back just in time for the congregation to get up for the benediction. We exited without visiting the folks! It was instructive to see how others worshiped. In visiting a congregation that practiced communion every Sunday I very much enjoyed the smoothness with which the sacrament was administered. I have many times been uneasy in our own setting because of the continuing change of pattern that leaves me anxious about what is to happen next. At the same time I noticed in the congregation that practiced it every Sunday that many persons appeared to have it in "automatic" and didn't seem to be engaged in the meaning of the symbols.

(Our family at Opryland – 2008)

In the summer of 2008 almost all of the family met at the Opryland Hotel in Nashville to celebrate our sixtieth wedding anniversary. We had a fabulous time, capping it with a visit to the Grand Ole Opry to hear a live performance. It was not front and center for our kind of music but it was a worthwhile time in connecting to a performance of another genre. We felt some reticence about spending a lot of money on what borders on decadence. Was this a proper venue for our family in light of all the important things you could do? It reminded me of a time while at the Hesston Corporation when I told my secretary that I wanted to see all of the travel expenses that were *out of line*. She had grown up poor and was still poor and she replied, "They're all *out of line*. I'll show you the ones that I believe you think are out of line."

Before Christmas 2005 Micah and Sarah were married in California. All of our children and grandchildren were there except John and Chris. Chris had both knees replaced the week before the wedding and even she could not make the trip that quickly after surgery! The wedding was a lovely event with two committed Christian young folks finding each other and deciding to sanctify their commitment in marriage. Ben was serving with MCC in Honduras and wanted to make the scene so we gave him the plane ticket to make the trip. It was worth it!

In May 2008 Ben married Jessica Sweigert in her parents' yard. A large white tent was erected for the occasion and they had a wonderful service complete with the singing of a couple hymns that really rocked the tent. Martha, just two weeks from hip replacement surgery, led the singing with a walker in front of her *just in case*. After the ceremony the crowd went down the road for a sit-down dinner in the Leatherman barn. Jessica was working as a delivery nurse at Wesley Medical Center in Wichita and Ben was working on completing his teaching degree at Wichita State. We were overjoyed for them both. As of this writing they have been blest with a bouncing son Christian. He is a *great* grandson.

June 27, 2009 marked the date for the marriage of Laura to Brent Sachs at Mishawaka, IN. The ceremony took place in Brent's back yard, a lovely setting for a solemn occasion. Mark, Beth and Saundra did a lot of the work to cater the meal for the 100+ guests. They honeymooned in Puerto Rico at the house owned by Ron and Esther Graber. They are a happily married couple.

Some have wondered about our decision to move to a retirement community when we were *only seventy* but it was the right move for us. It has also been important that we stay connected to our church family. A winter home or summer home has not been of interest to us because we need to be close to our church family and stay involved. This has been part of our life blood and we trust can continue to be as long as the Lord gives us sound minds and good enough bodies to make the scene. We have no quarrel with those who have a different viewpoint. We have enough difficulty finding our things with only one location to look for them!

The time beyond my working years has been filled more with watching what others are doing than actually doing something myself. We watch with interest the various pursuits of our children and grandchildren and great grandchildren. There have been high points and low points for all of them as we have rejoiced with them and wept with them. They have been and continue to be *very* extraordinary to us. We won't go into any details regarding their honors and achievements since those honors and achievements are their stories, not ours.

Some additional Musings

I have been extremely blest. A visiting minister at Whitestone asked for comments from the audience on a definition of "Wisdom." My good friend Wayne Swartzendruber responded with "Choosing the path of least regrets." It is not that I have always chosen that path but in the sum total of my life I can truly say the Lord was with me *all* the way. I understand only dimly what is meant by the "Grace of God." My particular friend and brother-in-law John W. Snyder said "Part of the grace of God is that God keeps us from knowing the future. We do not know the end from the beginning." My father would say, "We don't know what the future holds but we know who holds the future." A song that we sang in choir was particularly poignant to me in the wedding of words and music: "By Grace I choose the nobler part and turn my face to Thee." Even the decision to follow the path of obedience is a grace given.

When I look back on the part of my life I remember I am impressed again at how the Lord leads in the very small things that have helped shape and change my life. How I was led to the love of my life, Martha, and the wonderful and loving companion that she has been to me. After over sixty years together the love light has not dimmed. The gift God gave us in our children, grandchildren and great grandchildren, all gifts from Him.

In looking back I clearly see His hand in leading me in my life's work—preparing me for one only to lead me in a different direction. Giving me grace to do the job even when I felt uncomfortable and ill prepared to do it. He gave me strength to show up a few times even when I felt like hiding.

I am especially thankful for a sense of humor and a wife who laughs at my attempts to make the world a happier place. I try not to take myself too seriously. My father-in-law used to talk about "Looking at life with a jaundiced eye." I view this as just a *little* more righteous than being a cynic which I have also been accused of. There are many things I have dealt with during my lifetime which refused to be fixed in spite of my best effort. The first part of the Serenity Prayer penned by Reinhold Niebuhr has been a part of my life (passed on by Brother Glenn) for many years and has been a way I have looked at life and its ambiguities.

"God grant me the serenity to accept the things I cannot change; courage to change the things I can; and wisdom to know the difference."

How do we find the wisdom to sort it all out?

So I'm still asking questions. I have some answers to the questions I was raising during my long life but I still don't know if Beulah was older than Prince or if Prince was older than Beulah! I think I have the answer to the question with which I opened the book. There are times when duty calls us to do things which are not comfortable or convenient but we follow where the Lord leads. And sometimes things happen which don't fit easily within our frame of reference but we attempt to accept them within the providence of God.

One day all of the questions will be answered, so until then we do what we need to do. Live life to the fullest in the way the Lord leads. Sometime we'll understand.

And THAT'S THAT!

Epilogue

Following is a pictorial story of what our family currently looks like and just a bit about what each one is doing.

Howard and Martha as we looked in December, 2010

John Howard and his wife Christine (Petrocci) Hershberger live in rural Inman, KS. They are self-employed and have a company called *Sweetwater Farms* that produces alfalfa and bean sprouts, for distribution in a five-state area. They have two important avocations: the first is production of art work in various forms by Chris; and the other is Italian cooking primarily carried on by John. They regularly entertain groups at their home for an authentic Italian feast. They do not have any children.

(Jana, Marla, Felicity, Dan, Julie, Olivia, Sarah, Micah, Annalie & Joe)

Daniel Glenn and his wife Marla (Mullet) Hershberger live in Spring Hill, TN. Dan, with a couple partners, owns a company called *Integrity*. They produce health food supplements for a wide range of companies. They import their products, analyze them and prepare them for retail by combining ingredients and bottle or encapsulate them for their customers. Most of what they manufacture is sold under other brand names than their own. Marla enjoys the domestic pursuits of sewing, gardening, reading and taking care of grandchildren. They have three children: Jana, the oldest, is a registered nurse and is employed at a hospital in greater Nashville, TN. Julie is married to Joe Young, a pastor of a church in Great Falls, MT. They have four children: Annalie, Olivia, Felicity and Thomas (not pictured). Micah is married to Sarah (Langenbacher) and is an underwriter for an insurance company in Nashville. Sarah is a nanny and bread baker. She is hoping to be a stay at home mom in the future.

(Sam, Ben, Christian, Jessica, Phil & Diana)

Philip Earl and his wife Diana (Bergey) Hershberger live in Topeka, KS. He is a self-employed artist. Currently he also is buying houses and renovating them for resale. Diana is a special education teacher in the Topeka school system as well as a professional volunteer and gardener. They have two sons. Ben is married to Jessica (Sweigart) and they have a son Christian. Ben has just completed his teacher training at Wichita State University and has a contract to teach in Washington Elementary in McPherson, KS. Jessica is a registered nurse and is employed as a delivery nurse at the Newton Medical Center. Sam is working with his dad in house renovation.

(Daniel, Faith, Tim, Jessica)

Faith Lucille and her husband Tim Penner live in Harper, Kansas. He is principal owner and president of Harper Industries mentioned elsewhere in my story. Faith works primarily in volunteer assignments in the church and community. They have two children. Jessica is working for *Plowshares* in distribution in a voluntary service assignment in St. Louis. Daniel is a junior at Goshen College.

(Brent, Laura, Saundra, Beth, Mark)

Beth Anne and her husband Mark Goertz live in rural Inman, Kansas. He owns and operates a business known as *Inman Excavating.* They have two children. Laura is married to Brent Sachs. Laura is a Financial Sales Consultant for PNC Bank in Elkhart, IN. Brent is a personal trainer at a Mishawaka, IN Fitness club. Saundra owns a grocery store in Inman, KS. Beth is kept busy working for both her husband's and daughter's businesses.